# SHEPHERD'S NOTES

# SHEPHERD'S NOTES

*When you need a guide through the Scriptures*

# *Luke*

BROADMAN
&HOLMAN
PUBLISHERS

Nashville, Tennessee

© 1998

by Broadman & Holman Publishers

Nashville, Tennessee

All rights reserved

Printed in the United States of America

0–8054–9004–3

Dewey Decimal Classification: 226.4

Subject Heading: BIBLE. N.T. LUKE

Library of Congress Card Catalog Number: 97–37018

**Library of Congress Cataloging-in-Publication Data**

Luke / Dana Gould, editor

      p.  cm. — (Shepherd's notes)

    Includes bibliographical references.

    ISBN 0–8054–9004–3

    1. Bible. N.T. Luke—Study and teaching.    I. Gould, Dana.  1951–.

  II. Series

BS2596.L85   1998

  226.4'07—dc21                                97–37018

                                                 CIP

1 2 3 4 5 6   03 02 01 00 99 98

# CONTENTS

# FOREWORD

Dear Reader:

*Shepherd's Notes* are designed to give you a quick, step-by-step overview of every book of the Bible. They are not meant to be substitutes for the biblical text; rather, they are study guides intended to help you explore the wisdom of Scripture in personal or group study and to apply that wisdom successfully in your own life.

*Shepherd's Notes* guide you through the main themes of each book of the Bible and illuminate fascinating details through appropriate commentary and reference notes. Historical and cultural background information brings the Bible into sharper focus.

Six different icons, used throughout the series, call your attention to historical-cultural information, Old Testament and New Testament references, word pictures, unit summaries, and personal application for everyday life.

Whether you are a novice or a veteran at Bible study, I believe you will find *Shepherd's Notes* a resource that will take you to a new level in your mining and applying the riches of Scripture.

In Him,

David R. Shepherd
Editor-in-Chief

# HOW TO USE THIS BOOK

## DESIGNED FOR THE BUSY USER

*Shepherd's Notes* for Luke is designed to provide an easy-to-use tool for getting a quick handle on this Bible book's important features, and for gaining an understanding of its message. Information available in more difficult-to-use reference works has been incorporated into the *Shepherd's Notes* format. This brings you the benefits of many advanced and expensive works packed into one small volume.

*Shepherd's Notes* are for laymen, pastors, teachers, small-group leaders, and participants, as well as the classroom student. Enrich your personal study or quiet time. Shorten your class or small group preparation time as you gain valuable insights into the truths of God's Word that you can pass along to your students or group members.

## DESIGNED FOR QUICK ACCESS

Bible students with time constraints will especially appreciate the timesaving features built into the *Shepherd's Notes*. All features are intended to aid a quick and concise encounter with the heart of the message.

*Concise Commentary.* Luke's narrative is replete with characters, places, events, and instruction to believers. Short sections provide quick "snapshots" of sections of his narrative, highlighting important points and other information.

*Outlined Text.* A comprehensive outline covers the entire text of Luke's narrative. This is a valuable feature for following the narrative's flow, allowing for a quick, easy way to locate a particular passage.

*Shepherd's Notes.* These summary statements appear at the close of every key section of the narrative. While functioning in part as a quick summary, they also deliver the essence of the message presented in the sections which they cover.

*Icons.* Various icons in the margin highlight recurring themes in Luke and aid in selective searching or tracing of those themes.

*Sidebars and Charts.* These specially selected features provide additional background information to your study or preparation. These include definitions as well as cultural, historical, and biblical insights.

*Maps.* These are placed at appropriate places in the book to aid your understanding and study of a text or passage.

*Questions to Guide Your Study.* These thought-provoking questions and discussion starters are designed to encourage interaction with the truth and principles of God's Word.

## DESIGNED TO WORK FOR YOU

*Personal Study.* Using the *Shepherd's Notes* with a passage of Scripture can enlighten your study and take it to a new level. At your fingertips is information that would require searching several volumes to find. In addition, many points of application occur throughout the volume, contributing to personal growth.

*Teaching.* Outlines frame the text of Luke, providing a logical presentation of the message. Capsule thoughts designated as "Shepherd's Notes" provide summary statements for presenting the essence of key points and events. Application icons point out personal application of Luke's message, and Historical Context icons indicate where background information is supplied.

*Group Study.* *Shepherd's Notes* can be an excellent companion volume to use for gaining a quick but accurate understanding of the message of a Bible book. Each group member can benefit by having his or her own copy. The *Note's* format accommodates the study of or the tracing of Luke's themes throughout the narrative. Leaders may use its flexible features to prepare for group sessions or use them during group sessions. "Questions to Guide Your Study" can spark discussion of Luke's key points and truths.

## LIST OF MARGIN ICONS USED IN LUKE

*Shepherd's Notes.* Placed at the end of each section, a capsule statement that provides the reader with the essence of the message of that section.

*Old Testament Reference.* Used when the writer refers to Old Testament Scripture passages that are related or have a bearing on the passage's understanding or interpretation.

*New Testament Reference.* Used when the writer refers to New Testament passages that are related to or have a bearing on the passage's understanding or interpretation.

*Historical Background.* To indicate historical, cultural, geographical, or biographical information that sheds light on the understanding or interpretation of a passage.

*Personal Application.* Used when the text provides a personal or universal application of truth.

*Word Picture.* Indicates that the meaning of a specific word or phrase is illustrated so as to shed light on it.

Luke's Gospel is the longest single book of the New Testament. Luke wrote as a Christian historian. He intended that his Gospel and Acts serve as a single volume dealing with the beginning and growth of the early church.

## AUTHOR

The authorship of Luke was never disputed until the second half of the nineteenth century. Yet it should be observed that Luke and Acts are two of the nine books in the New Testament that are anonymous. Neither Acts nor Luke names its author; but since the second century, church tradition has identified Luke as the author of Luke-Acts.

## AUDIENCE

Luke was explicitly written to Theophilus (1:1–4). Theophilus appears to have had some exposure to the faith, as Luke's introduction makes clear. In fact, it is quite likely that Theophilus was a Gentile believer struggling with his association in a movement that had Jewish origins.

## PURPOSE

Luke wrote his Gospel for a variety of reasons that includes the following:

1. Luke wanted to confirm the message of God's promise and salvation through Jesus.
2. He wished to portray God's faithfulness both to Israel and to all persons while explaining why so many in Israel tragically rejected Jesus.
3. He wanted to lay the foundation in Luke for his defense in Acts of the full

The Gospel of Luke and the Book of Acts were both addressed to Theophilus (Acts 1:1), whose name means "friend of God." All we know about Theophilus is found in these two verses. The words *most excellent* suggest that he was a person of authority, perhaps a government official. Theophilus may have been a convert who had been taught many things about Christ, or he may have been an open-minded seeker who had heard these things. Luke wrote so that Theophilus would know the truth and certainty of the Christian gospel.

Paul referred to Luke as "our dear friend . . . the doctor" (Col. 4:14). During Paul's last imprisonment in Rome, he wrote to Timothy: "Only Luke is with me" (2 Tim. 4:11).

membership of Gentiles as part of God's people and promise.

4. He wished to offer a word of reconciliation and explanation to Jews by showing how responding to Jesus was the natural fulfillment of God's promises to Israel.

5. He wished to show that God's promise extends to all people by showing the variety of social classes and people who responded to Jesus.

## DATE AND PLACE OF WRITING

*Date.* The date when Luke was written cannot be established with certainty. Luke wrote his own introduction (1:1–4) which indicates that he was not the first to make a written record of God's revelation in Christ. Most biblical scholars believe that both Luke and Matthew drew on Mark's Gospel in writing theirs. It seems likely that Luke was written before Acts, since Acts is part two of Luke.

Acts ends before the outcome of Paul's appeal to Caesar is known. This would have been in the early 60s. On this view, Luke would have been written prior to 60 and thus Mark all the earlier.

*Place of writing.* The most probable origin of Luke is Rome. Luke reached Rome in Paul's company and was in Rome when Paul wrote Colossians and Philemon during Paul's first Roman imprisonment (A.D. 59–62). The circumstances would have allowed time for the composition of Luke-Acts.

## LITERARY FORM

Luke is a Gospel, a form unique to the Bible. The account operates like a narrative. It is more than a biography because it is selective and has a theological message to convey. It is a history, but only a selective history. We are told nothing

"We can be fairly certain of the circumstances in which Luke learned of these events. Having come to Jerusalem, with Paul just before the latter was arrested, and being on hand to accompany him again when he was eventually sent away from Caesarea on the voyage to Rome, Luke presumably stayed in Palestine for the two-year period of his friend's imprisonment, and without doubt used the opportunity to gather material for his Gospel. Behind chapters 1 and 2 in particular there must surely lie long conversations between him and Mary."

Michael Wilcock, *Savior of the World: The Message of Luke's Gospel*, (Leicester: InterVarsity Press, 1979), 42.

about the details of Jesus' childhood. Rather, we move from Jesus' birth directly to His ministry with only one incident from the age of twelve and the ministry of John the Baptist intervening briefly. A Gospel is a theological, pastoral explanation of the significance and impact of Jesus' life, death, and resurrection. So characters, setting, movements of time and location, mood, and the arrangement of events are all a part of telling the account of Jesus' ministry.

## BASIC OUTLINE OF LUKE'S GOSPEL
   I. John the Baptist and Jesus (1:1—2:52)
  II. Preparation for Ministry (3:1—4:13)
 III. Galilean Ministry (4:14—9:50)
 IV. Jerusalem Journey (9:51—19:44)
  V. Final Ministry in Jerusalem (19:45—24:53)

## QUESTIONS TO GUIDE YOUR STUDY
  1. Why did Luke write his Gospel?
  2. Where did Luke get his material for writing his Gospel? Explain the relationship between Luke and Acts.
  3. What are some of the distinctives and unique themes of Luke's Gospel?

Taken from Robert H. Stein, *Luke*, vol. 24, New American Commentary
(Nashville, Tenn.: Broadman & Holman Publishers, 1994), p. 61

# LUKE 1

- - - - - - - - - - - - - - - - - - - -

Luke's Gospel begins with a literary prologue that ranks among the best Greek literature of the first century. Numerous parallels of such a prologue exist in the Jewish and Hellenistic literature of that period.

## PROLOGUE (1:1–4)

Luke's main purpose for the prologue was to establish his credibility as a historian. He sought to do this in 1:3 by compounding terms that reveal his care and expertise in writing.

### The Period in Which the Gospels Were Written (vv. 1–2)

Verse 1 reveals that Luke was not the first to write about what God in Christ had caused to be accomplished among the believers.

Very likely many of the writings were not what might be called complete accounts of the coming, teachings, ministry, death, and resurrection of Jesus. Many of the early writings probably were about only one or perhaps a few aspects of the gospel.

### The Writing of Luke's Gospel (vv. 3–4)

Luke did not include everything about Jesus in his Gospel. He, like other Gospel writers, was selective in what he recorded. He was a writer and witness, not just a compiler. Everything he had found in his careful research did not become part of his book, only what fitted his purpose.

*■ Luke's main purpose for writing the pro-*
*■ logue was to establish his credibility. It was*
*■ the first step to accomplishing his goal for*
*■ writing his Gospel, which was to help his*
*■ readers become certain of the truthfulness of*
*■ the gospel teachings the readers had been*
*■ taught. Although a careful historian, Luke*

Mark's Gospel was probably one of the writings that preceded Luke. The essence of over 50 percent of the verses in Mark is found in Luke. The percentage of Mark in Matthew is even higher—about 90 percent.

■ *made no secret of his faith and of his purpose*
■ *to seek to persuade others to have faith*
■ *in Christ.*

## JOHN THE BAPTIST'S BIRTH ANNOUNCED (1:5–25)

Luke moves from prologue to two important birth announcements. Zechariah and Elizabeth, the parents of John the Baptist, represent the true piety that existed in Israel. They were righteous in the best sense of the word They believed in and practiced prayer; they hoped for the coming of the Messiah.

Zechariah was offering incense in the Temple when the angel appeared to him. Zechariah responded to the angel with a question reminiscent of Abraham's words under similar circumstances (v. 18; Gen. 15:8), but he lacked Abraham's faith. The angel's prophecy must have seemed too good to be true, as he responded with the question, "How can I be sure of this?" Because of his unbelief, Zechariah was struck dumb until John's birth. Elizabeth viewed her childlessness as a stigma; therefore, she rejoiced when she realized she was pregnant. She already was experiencing, in anticipation, the joy and gladness of which Gabriel spoke.

■ *Gabriel announced to Zechariah that he*
■ *would be the father of the prophet who would*
■ *call people to repentance before the coming*
■ *of the Lord.*

## JESUS' BIRTH ANNOUNCED (1:26–38)

Having just described the announcement of John the Baptist's birth, Luke proceeds with a description of the announcement of Jesus' birth.

An angel appeared to Mary, a virgin, and announced that she would give birth to Jesus. Unlike Zechariah, she responds with trust and submission to God's will.

This account of Jesus' birth has a number of parallel's with John's birth: the mention of the sixth month and two of the main characters, the angel Gabriel and Elizabeth.

- ■ *The mighty work God had done in John the*
- ■ *Baptist's conception would be surpassed by an*
- ■ *even greater miracle in the virginal concep-*
- ■ *tion of Jesus. In addition, the mighty work*
- ■ *God foretold He would do through John the*
- ■ *Baptist's ministry would be surpassed by an*
- ■ *even greater work through His Son's ministry.*

## THE MEETING OF JOHN THE BAPTIST AND JESUS (1:39–56)

### *Elizabeth's Prophecy (vv. 39–45)*

Mary hastened to visit her kinswoman Elizabeth. As soon as Mary greeted her, Elizabeth was filled with the Spirit and spoke as a prophet. She referred to Mary as "the mother of my Lord" (v. 43) and blessed her for believing God's word. This scene thus reinforced the theme of superiority of Mary's son to Elizabeth's son.

Elizabeth's words in verse 42, like Gabriel's in verse 28, were used in later centuries to exalt Mary to a divine-like role of her own. This misses the point not only of these passages but also of the whole New Testament. Mary was the recipient of grace, not a source of grace. Her blessedness was the blessedness of one who became a willing channel of divine blessings to others.

### Mary's Song (vv. 46–56)

Mary's response in verses 46–55 reflects humble trust. This passage is a kind of hymnlike poem—often called the Magnificat.

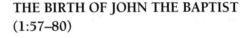

■ *In this passage we see several of Luke's*
■ *major emphases. First is the theme of rever-*
■ *sal. The humble are exalted, and the arro-*
■ *gant are brought low. Second, we see the*
■ *fulfillment of prophecy and the divine prom-*
■ *ises. Third, we gain an understanding of*
■ *Mary's offspring. The child born of Mary*
■ *was clearly greater than the child born of*
■ *Elizabeth.*

## THE BIRTH OF JOHN THE BAPTIST (1:57–80)

### His Name Is John (vv. 57–66)

Neighbors and relatives assumed the child of Elizabeth and Zechariah would be named for his father, but Zechariah and Elizabeth remembered the angel's words and named him John. All of this was done in such a way that everyone who heard it was impressed. They wondered what special destiny awaited this child: "What then is this child going to be?"

### Light in the Darkness (vv. 67–79)

Now Zechariah was filled with the Spirit and prophesied of the new day about to dawn. His poem or song is often called the *Benedictus*. The first half of the song (vv. 68–75) wove together several Old Testament promises that stand fulfilled in the Messiah's coming.

**Naming of Children**

In biblical tradition, the task of naming a child generally fell to the mother (Gen. 29:31—30:24; 1 Sam. 1:20), but could be performed by the father, and in exceptional cases by nonparental figures. The biblical concept of naming was rooted in the ancient world's understanding that a name expressed essence. To know the name of a person was to know that person's total character and nature. Revealing character and destiny, personal names might express hopes for the child's future. Changing of names could occur at divine or human initiative, revealing a transformation in character or destiny.

*In the Wilderness (v. 80)*
Luke summed up John's childhood in this single verse. The last part of the verse is laden with anticipation. John went into the wilderness. Later the word of the Lord would come to him in the wilderness, and he would begin his call for repentance.

■ *Luke wanted his readers to understand*
■ *Zechariah's divinely inspired hymn as prais-*
■ *ing God for fulfilling His promises to His*
■ *people and describing the roles of John the*
■ *Baptist and especially the Messiah.*

## QUESTIONS TO GUIDE YOUR STUDY

1. Describe Luke's prologue. How does it relate to his goals for writing his Gospel?
2. Compare the births of John and Jesus. What parallels do we see? What contrasts does Luke make?
3. What is the significance of Mary's song?
4. What truths does Zechariah's hymn present? Why would its message be significant to the people of Israel?

## LUKE 2

## THE BIRTH OF JESUS (2:1–20)
Next follows Luke's narrative of Jesus' birth.

*The Fullness of Time (vv. 1–7)*
Luke's purpose in mentioning Caesar Augustus's decree probably was to show that God moves in the affairs of nations to accomplish His purposes. The Caesars appeared to be in control of

Augustus Caesar ruled as emperor over most of the civilized world. He was honored as a great benefactor. Under his reign the world enjoyed a period of peace. This passage in Luke told of the coming one who would offer the kind of peace that lay beyond the power of the most powerful man on earth.

**Savior, Christ, Lord**

Luke used three titles to describe Jesus. Each was steeped in Old Testament Scriptures and rich in meaning for Luke's readers.

*Savior* means healer, deliverer, benefactor. *Christ* means Messiah, the anointed one to rule as king in fulfillment of God's promises to David. *Lord* speaks of the divine nature of the One who was born.

These three titles also appear together in Phil. 3:20.

human destiny; but God was at work through all these events, working out His eternal purposes.

### Heaven Touches Earth (vv. 8–14)

At many points in Luke 1:5–2:52, signs herald the divine intervention into history, but none is more dramatic than the angels' announcement to the shepherds on the night of Jesus' birth. Three verses focus on the significance of this unique event: 10, 11, and 14.

Verse 10 is the angels' announcement of "good news of great joy that will be for all people." This was the first public announcement of the good news of Jesus' birth.

Verse 11 focuses on the one whose coming was heralded. Each of the three titles—Savior, Christ, and Lord—has significant meaning:

Verse 14 has been translated various ways. It is best to translate this verse as it is found in the NIV or the NRSV. A paraphrase of this passage might be, "Peace to people who are the objects of God's good will" (Robert J. Dean, *Luke*, Broadman & Holman, p. 27).

### Witnesses of the Good News (vv. 15–20)

The shepherds were not only the first to hear the proclamation of the good news, but they were the first humans to tell others.

■ By conveying the historical setting and cir-
■ cumstances of Jesus' birth, Luke reinforced
■ two of his themes: (1) that Jesus was the ful-
■ fillment of the Jewish messianic hopes; and
■ (2) God's sovereignty over history.

# LIGHT TO THE GENTILES AND GLORY TO ISRAEL (2:21–39)

The Temple was central in Israel's worship and hopes. We find it prominent in this chapter of Luke's narrative (vv. 22–38, 41–51). In this particular section, Luke 2:22–38 tells how Jesus was presented in the Temple as an infant.

### *According to the Law (vv. 21–24)*

Five times in this episode Luke mentions that Mary and Joseph acted according to the Law (vv. 22, 23, 24, 27, 39).

### *The Shadow of the Cross (vv. 25–39)*

Three times the passage refers to the Spirit's influence on Simeon, a devout man living in Jerusalem at the time of Jesus' birth. Simeon was seeking the fulfillment of messianic prophecy when Israel would be restored. God promised Simeon that he would not die before seeing the Christ. When Joseph and Mary brought Jesus to the Temple for purification rites, Simeon blessed God for allowing him to see God's salvation. This salvation would be not only glory for Israel but also light for the revelation to the Gentiles.

Simeon warned that Jesus would cause both the "falling" and "rising" of many in Israel.

A prophetess, Anna, also recognized Jesus as the Messiah and thanked God for Him.

They performed three ceremonies prescribed by the Law: (1) they circumcised their eight-day-old son (Gen. 17:9–14); (2) Mary went to the Temple for purification as prescribed in Lev. 12:22–24; and (3) Mary and Joseph presented Jesus in the Temple following the instructions in Exod. 13:2, 12–15.

An important aspect of this passage is that it reveals that Jesus was born into a home of modest means but a home of deep loyalty to the religion of the Old Testament.

- Simeon's prediction (vv. 34–35) is the first
- connection in Luke between Jesus' mission
- and suffering. For the first time, the shadow
- of the cross fell across Jesus' life. Jesus is the
- salvation of God, but in the midst of hope is

**Feast of the Passover**

Passover was one of the three annual festivals that Jewish men were required to celebrate in Jerusalem (Deut. 16:16). Passover itself was the opening feast of the seven-day (or eight-day by another reckoning) festival called the Feast of Unleavened Bread and was celebrated on the fifteenth day of Nisan. The entire feast, however, was popularly called the Feast of Passover. Passover commemorated God's deliverance or exodus of His people out of Egypt and the death angel's passing over Israel's firstborn.

*the reality that fulfillment comes mixed with pain and suffering.*

## THE BOY JESUS IN THE TEMPLE (2:40–52)

Apart from the summary statements about Jesus' growth in 2:40 and 2:52, the only knowledge of Jesus' childhood comes from the episode recorded in 2:41–51.

Mary and Joseph attended the Feast of the Passover every year. When Jesus was twelve years of age, they brought Him along to the feast. When they returned home, the boy Jesus remained behind. When a concerned Mary and Joseph returned to Jerusalem looking for the missing boy, they were astonished to find Him in the Temple sitting among the teachers.

The teachers at the Temple were amazed at the careful attention, insightful questions, and wise answers of the boy from Nazareth.

Mary's anxious question and Jesus' answer are the heart of the passage. Jesus revealed an awareness of His unique relationship with His heavenly Father: "Didn't you know I had to be in my Father's house?"

As an obedient son, Jesus dutifully returned to Nazareth with His parents. In verse 52 Luke chronicles the development of Jesus intellectually ("in wisdom"), physically ("in stature"), spiritually ("favor with God"), and socially ("favor with man").

■ *This section, dominated by Old Testament*
■ *allusions, opens Luke's Gospel with notes of*
■ *fulfillment and indications of God's direc-*

- tion. *The brief glimpse of Jesus as a child that*
- *Luke provided forms a kind of bridge*
- *between the events connected with His birth*
- *and the account of His adult ministry.*

## QUESTIONS TO GUIDE YOUR STUDY

1. What unique aspects about Jesus' birth does Luke reveal with his infancy narrative?

2. What is significant about the prophecies of Simeon and Anna?

3. Luke is the only Gospel that records an event from Jesus' childhood. What insights about Jesus' growth and development can we glean from this brief account? Why do you think Luke included this passage?

## LUKE 3

### JOHN THE BAPTIST, A MAN WHOSE TIME HAD COME (3:1–6)

As in 2:1, Luke opened this account by tying the opening events of Jesus' ministry to contemporary history.

In 1:5 Luke began with the words "In the time of Herod king of Judea." Luke 2:12 mentions Caesar Augustus and Quirinius, the governor of Syria. Luke 3:1 dates the following events "in the fifteenth year of the reign of Tiberius Caesar."

Part of Luke's purpose for writing his Gospel was to help his readers date the events. He was writing a Gospel about a Savior for all people. He wanted Theophilus and other Gentile readers to see the events narrated as part of the fabric of a world shared by Jews and Gentiles alike.

Luke 3:2*b* brings John back into the picture after noting in 1:80 that he went to live in the wilderness.

**Baptism of Repentance**

Several New Testament texts refer to repentance, baptism, and forgiveness (see Acts 2:38). "Repentance" here literally means *a change of mind* but refers more broadly to the human involvement in the experience of conversion.

John not only preached repentance before the Lord's coming; he also signified this message with baptism. The Old Testament prophets had used various kinds of prophetic symbolism. John's prophetic sign was baptism. This was a way of signifying repentance and forgiveness.

## THE MISSION OF JOHN THE BAPTIST (3:7–20)

In this section Luke gives us three examples of John the Baptist's preaching.

### Example One: Baptism and Repentance (vv. 7–9)

John's message was repentance; baptism was its sign. The crowd had come for baptism. They obviously needed forgiveness. But John called some of them "a brood of vipers" and refused to baptize them because he saw no evidence of repentance. Without a change of heart, baptism would have been a farce. It was meaningful only as a sign of genuine repentance. Repentance, not baptism, is what brings forgiveness.

### Example Two: Changing How We Live (vv. 10–14)

There is a striking contrast between the people in verses 7–9 and those of verses 10–14. The former group presumed on their ancestry and did not repent. The latter group were typical of those who earnestly heeded John's call for repentance.

### Example Three: The Spirit and Fire (vv. 15–20)

Because John's activity aroused great interest and speculation, it was only natural that some wondered whether he was the Messiah. John quickly denied this. In his day, one of the duties of a slave was to remove his master's shoes.

Thus, John saw himself as a slave in comparison to the Messiah.

The phrases *from heaven* and *with you I am well pleased* are possible allusions to Ps. 2:7 and Isa. 42:1.

- *Alfred Plummer says of John the Baptist:*
- *"The whole man was a sermon." Luke*
- *3:1–20 shows how John was consumed with*
- *his awesome mission. Luke tells of his pro-*
- *phetic call, his message, his words about the*
- *Messiah, and his arrest.*

## JESUS' BAPTISM (3:21–22)

Luke's account of Jesus' baptism emphasized that it happened when all the people were being baptized. This showed His intent to identify with those He had come to serve and save.

## LUKE'S GENEALOGY (3:23–38)

This genealogy contains seventy-seven ancestors. The exact arrangement of generations, in contrast to what we find in Matthew, is uncertain.

It's likely that if all the facts were known, it would be clear why the two genealogies are different.

When a Gentile became a Jew, one of the requirements was a kind of baptism. The Gentile immersed himself in water as a part of his entrance rites into Judaism as a proselyte. John's baptism was different from the proselyte baptism in at least two ways. First, John did the baptism himself. Second, and more important, John's baptism had a strong moral and universal basis. Proselyte baptism assumed Gentiles were outsiders who needed to be baptized to become insiders. John's baptism assumed that everyone needed repentance to be an insider.

- *This section is a prelude to Jesus' public min-*
- *istry. It shows Jesus committing Himself to a*
- *mission of service and sacrifice. His geneal-*
- *ogy emphasizes His ties not only to Israel but*
- *also to all humanity.*

## QUESTIONS TO GUIDE YOUR STUDY

1. What is repentance? What must one do to truly repent?

2. Describe the universal nature of the gospel? Why was this a revolutionary concept among John's listeners?
3. What characterized the message of John's preaching?

## LUKE 4

Hebrews 4:15 said of Jesus that He was "tempted in every way, just as we are—yet was without sin." This statement underscores the reality of Jesus' temptations.

### TEMPTED AS WE ARE (4:1–13)

Jesus' temptations were like ours in that they were real, but His experience with temptation was unique in two ways:

1. He resisted temptation and did not sin.
2. He met temptation on the field of battle and emerged victorious.

The temptations themselves came from external sources, and in all three Jesus was obedient to God's will. The temptations were all messianic in nature and thus should be seen as a parallel to 1 John 2:16.

### *The First Temptation: Physical Needs (vv. 3–4)*

Jesus was tempted to use His power to meet physical needs. This was more than a temptation to feed Himself miraculously; it was a temptation to embark on a mission to feed hungry people.

"And He humbled you and let you be hungry, and fed you with manna which you did not know, nor did your fathers know, that He might make you understand that man does not live by bread alone, but man lives by everthing that proceeds out of the mouth of the Lord" (Deut. 8:3, NASB).

He resisted by quoting Deut. 8:3.

### *The Second Temptation: Power (vv. 5–8)*

Jesus' second temptation was to seek the power of a world ruler. The subtle appeal of the temptation—like the other two—was that it matched popular expectations about the Messiah.

Again Jesus resisted by quoting Deut. 6:13.

### The Third Temptation: Popularity (vv. 9–12)

The third temptation was to perform a dazzling miracle in the Temple. Many people were anxiously awaiting a Messiah who would perform spectacular signs.

Once again Jesus quoted Scripture, this time Deut. 6:16.

"You shall fear only the Lord your God; and you shall worshp Him, and swear by His name" (Deut. 6:13, NASB).

"You shall not put the Lord your God to the test, as you tested Him at Massah" (Deut. 6:16, NASB).

■ *Throughout His temptations, Jesus found*
■ *His answers in the Scriptures. He was armed*
■ *with the "sword of the Spirit" (Eph. 6:17) for*
■ *His battle with the devil. His being "full of*
■ *the Spirit" is a model for the believer.*

### JESUS' MINISTRY IN GALILEE IN MINIATURE (4:14–30)

### A Good Start (vv. 14–15)

Luke began his portrayal of Jesus' ministry with the account of Jesus' first sermon, and in it Luke provided his readers with Jesus' own description of His mission and ministry.

### A Mission to the People (vv. 16–21)

This is one of the earliest records of what took place in a Jewish synagogue service. As was the custom, Jesus stood to read the Scriptures and sat to teach.

### His Own Received Him Not (vv. 22–30)

The initial reaction of Jesus' hearers was favorable. But as He continued, they began to wonder and raise questions in their minds. They wondered at the discrepancy between the man and His message.

Jesus, sensing their skepticism, used two proverbs to illustrate their feelings:

"The Spirit of the Lord God is upon me, Because the Lord has anointed me
 To bring good news to the afflicted;
 He has sent me to bind up the brokenhearted,
 To proclaim liberty to captives,
 And freedom to prisoners;
 To proclaim the favorable year of the Lord,
 And the day of vengeance of our God;
 To comfort all who mourn" (Isa. 61:1–2, NASB).

**Proverb**

This word is translated from the Greek term *parabole*, which has a broad range of meaning from story and example parables, allegories, similitudes, and metaphors to proverbs. This particular proverb has numerous parallels both in form and in context. For context, see Luke 23:35. For form, we find in Greek literature, "Physician, physician heal thine own limp!" Here as elsewhere (Luke 5:22; 6:8; 7:40; 9:47; 11:17) Jesus possessed a unique awareness of others' thoughts.

**Kingdom of God**

Verse 43 is the first occurrence of the expression *kingdom of God* in Luke. As he anticipated that his readers already possessed some understanding of its meaning, Luke made no attempt to define the expression.

- "Physician, heal yourself!"
- "No prophet is accepted in his hometown."

These proverbs were Jesus' way of responding to their demand for signs among His own neighbors. His ministry, which was as broad as human need, could not be confined to His hometown, nor even to His own nation. They became so angry that they ran Jesus out of town and even tried to kill Him.

■ *Luke records the earliest days of Jesus'*
■ *Galilean ministry, which centered in the syn-*
■ *agogues of Galilee. Initially, Jesus was popu-*
■ *lar and well received by His audience. But*
■ *soon He was greeted with skepticism.*

**THE POWER OF THE AUTHORITATIVE WORD (4:31–44)**

Luke records four incidents in this section that take place in Capernaum, a kind of home base for His Galilean ministry. Here Jesus shows his power over demons and physical diseases.

■ *Two major themes of Luke emerge in this*
■ *section. First, Jesus performed miracles that*
■ *were examples of His power and authority.*
■ *Second, Luke clarifies for his readers how*
■ *Jesus' self-proclaimed messianic mission is to*
■ *be interpreted.*

**QUESTIONS TO GUIDE YOUR STUDY**

1. Why is Jesus' victory over temptation such an encouragement for the believer? In what ways was His temptation differ-

ent than ours? What steps or precautions might believers take to equip themselves for resisting temptation?

2. Describe Jesus' mission as He began His Galilean ministry? How was He received?

3. What is a parable? Why did Jesus use them in His teaching?

4. What message did the miracles of Jesus convey to those who witnessed them?

# LUKE 5

## BASIC STEPS IN FOLLOWING JESUS (5:1–11)

### *Obedience (vv. 1–5)*

Simon Peter already had some kind of relationship with Jesus, but until this incident he was basically a fisherman. He fished as a business, not as a hobby; and he was good at it. He and his partners, James and John, were owners of a fishing business.

Jesus' command in verse 4 probably took Peter by surprise. His answer was typical of Peter's later responses to Jesus. He said what he thought, but ended up doing as Jesus commanded.

### *Confession (vv. 6–8)*

The miracle of the great shoal of fish overwhelmed not only Peter's nets and boats but also Peter himself. Peter asked Jesus to depart from him.

### *Commitment (vv. 9–11)*

Fortunately for Peter, Jesus did not go away. Instead, He spoke words of comfort and chal-

"Fishermen made a better-than-average income (even if they had a bad night...), so leaving their job is an act of radical commitment that they would expect to adversely affect them economically."

Craig S. Keener in *The Bible Background Commentary: New Testament* (Downers Grove: InterVarsity Press, 1993), 201.

lenge. He dealt kindly with Peter's fear and agitated spirit. He then called Peter to become a different kind of fisherman. No longer was he to catch fish; now he was to catch human beings.

Peter's response was total commitment. Giving up his business to follow Jesus was not easy, but his experience with Jesus brought him to the point of commitment. He cut his ties with the past. From now on he would follow Jesus.

■ *Those who would follow Jesus must embrace*
■ *the basic steps: obedience, confession, and*
■ *commitment. When Peter cut his ties to the*
■ *past, it was the first step in his pilgrimage as*
■ *a disciple. There can be no pilgrimage with-*
■ *out a beginning.*

## JESUS HEALS A LEPER (5:12–16)

No group in ancient society was more pitiful than lepers. Their disease was a slow, lingering death. They died inch by inch. To make matters worse, lepers were cut off from the rest of society, including their families. Nothing but a corpse was worse than a leper. Yet Jesus dared to touch the leper and to speak the authoritative word that caused him to be cured.

## BLASPHEMY (5:17–26)

### A Delegation of Dignitaries (v. 17)

Pharisees and teachers of the law showed up to hear and observe Jesus. They came from all over Galilee and Judea, including Jerusalem itself. Luke mentions no sinister intent, but these religious leaders became Jesus' severest critics.

**Pharisees**

The teachers of the Law who opposed Jesus were comprised primarily of the Pharisees. They were the most influential of the three major Jewish sects (the other two being the Sadducees and Essenes). We first read of them in the second century B.C.

They believed in a strict keeping of the Law, as interpreted in their own traditions. They were separatists who sought to avoid contact with unclean things and unclean people. The "teachers of the law," or scribes, were professional students of the Law, and most of them were Pharisees.

### Sins Forgiven (vv. 18–20)

A paralytic was brought to Jesus for healing. To bypass the crowd surrounding Jesus, the men who brought the paralytic went onto the roof and lowered him through the tiles into the middle of the crowd in front of Jesus. He forgave the paralytic of his sins and then healed him.

### Blasphemer or Savior? (vv. 21–26)

The scribes and Pharisees began accusing Jesus of blasphemy. He was claiming to do something only God can do—forgive sins.

The people who witnessed the miracle responded with praise for God's grace for the paralytic. "Awe" or fear is a common response by those who witness God's power.

■ *The testimony of the New Testament is that*
■ *Jesus was without sin. His opponents, how-*
■ *ever, accused Him of several "sins." Because*
■ *Jesus claimed to do something only God can*
■ *do (forgive a man's sins), the scribes and*
■ *Pharisees accused Him of blasphemy. In con-*
■ *trast to the religious leaders, the crowd was*
■ *amazed at Jesus' miracle of healing and gave*
■ *praise to God.*

## ASSOCIATING WITH SINNERS (5:27–32)

Luke presents Jesus as the friend of sinners. Jesus freely associated with all kinds of people. This placed Him on a collision course with the Pharisees.

In response to His critics, Jesus used the analogy of the physician who went where the sick people were.

The tax collectors were outcasts from respectable society. They were collaborators with a foreign government. They had daily contact with all kinds of other "unclean" people. The word *sinners* here means the common people who paid little heed to the religious scruples of the Pharisees.

*True Christianity has always broken down economic, social, ethnic, and racial barriers.*

## NEGLECTING RELIGIOUS DISCIPLINES (5:33–39)

### Fast or Feast? (vv. 33–35)

Pious Pharisees fasted twice each week. They apparently viewed fasting as a mark of special commitment and dedication. They criticized Jesus' disciples for not fasting.

Jesus explained that fasting during a wedding is inappropriate. The Bible refers to the messianic age as a wedding feast.

### The Old and the New (vv. 36–39)

Jesus broadened His application with another analogy, which Luke calls a parable. The issue was the relationship between the new way of Jesus and the old way of Judaism. Jesus' way simply cannot be "patched" onto Judaism like a piece of cloth.

■ *The human response to the gospel is one of*
■ *Luke's strong emphases. Jesus' mission*
■ *included several calls: (1) a call for sinners*
■ *to repent; (2) a call to follow Jesus; and (3)*
■ *a call that addressed the outcasts.*

## QUESTIONS TO GUIDE YOUR STUDY

1. Jesus freely associated with the outcasts of His day. What are some ways we might implement His example in our society?

**Wineskins**

Wine making has always been a major industry in Syria-Palestine. In Old Testament times, the presses for making wine were usually cut or hewed out of rock and were connected to channels to lower rock-cut vats where the juice was allowed to collect. The juice was then poured into jars or wineskins. Wineskins were dehaired skins of small animals such as goats, which were sewn together to hold milk and wine. The point of Jesus' parable is the incompatibility of the old wineskin with the new wine. New wine, if placed in old wineskins, will destroy both skins and wine because as the new wine ferments, the old wineskin is not sufficiently pliable and will thus burst, spilling the wine.

2. What was Jesus' point regarding fasting? Why did the Pharisees take issue with Him?
3. Consider Jesus' parable of the old and the new wine. What made Judaism so inadequate to contain the new way of the gospel?

## LUKE 6

Jesus on occasion fasted, and He often spent time in prayer. However, He did not make fasting into a prescribed ritual. The kind of fasting He practiced was a natural fasting that resulted from preoccupation with more important matters (see John 4:31–34).

### BREAKING THE SABBATH (6:1–11)

#### *Lord of the Sabbath (vv. 1–5)*

Keeping the Sabbath was near the top of the list of Pharisaic virtues. As in other areas, the Pharisees had their own rigid definitions and requirements. They were determined to avoid even the appearance of working on the Sabbath.

Jesus kept the Sabbath as the Old Testament had intended, but He made no effort to conform to the rigid scruples of the Pharisees. He referred His critics to the example of David. When David was desperately hungry, he broke the law by eating the bread of the presence (vv. 3–4). If David could do this, how much more could the Son of David?

#### *Doing Good on the Sabbath (vv. 6–11)*

The original intent of the Sabbath was to provide a day of rest that would free people from the tyranny of a life of unending toil. God, therefore, instituted the Sabbath for the good of humanity.

Verse 11 describes the deep fury of Jesus' critics. They felt humiliated. Now they were more than critics; they were enemies.

Sabbath

The Sabbath is the day of rest, considered holy to God. It derives from God's rest on the seventh day following His creation of the universe. It was viewed as a sign of the covenant relation between God and His people and of the eternal rest which He promised them. The habit of Jesus was to observe the Sabbath as a day of worship in the synagogues, but His failure to comply with the minute restrictions of the Pharisaic observance of the law brought conflict and confrontation with the religious leaders of His day.

■ *In this section Jesus claimed that He, as Son*
■ *of Man, was Lord of the Sabbath. He also*
■ *manifested this authority by healing a man*
■ *on the Sabbath.*

## DISCIPLESHIP AS A WAY OF LIFE (6:12–49)

In this section, Jesus selected His closest followers and instructed them and His other disciples. Verses 20–49 make up what is sometimes called the Sermon on the Plain.

## CHOOSING OF THE TWELVE DISCIPLES (6:12–19)

The word *disciples* (v. 13) means "learners" or "followers" and refers to the larger group of Jesus' followers. The word *apostles* means "messengers sent out under the authority of another." The word was most often used later of those whom the risen Christ sent out as witnesses of His resurrection. The Twelve formed the core of these special witnesses. Luke noted that after Judas's death, a replacement was chosen.

Luke's account of the choosing of the Twelve emphasizes the all-night prayer that preceded the choice. The selection of the Twelve signified the new Israel that Jesus was creating. The twelve apostles corresponded to the twelve tribes of Israel.

| LISTS OF DISCIPLES IN THE NEW TESTAMENT |
| :---: |
| 1. Matthew 10:2–4 |
| 2. Mark 3:16–19 |
| 3. Luke 6:12–16 |
| 4. Acts 1:13 |

## THE SERMON ON THE PLAIN (6:20–49)

### *Beatitudes and Woes (vv. 20–26)*

Luke now introduced us to Jesus' second sermon (the first was recorded in 4:16–30).

Whereas His first was addressed to "crowds," this sermon He addressed to His disciples.

*Beatitudes.* The word *blessed* means "happy" or "fortunate." Jesus pronounced as blessed the poor, the hungry, the sad, and the persecuted.

*Woes.* Jesus also pronounced woes on the counterparts of the blessed: the rich, the well-fed, the merry, and the popular.

Here we find one of Luke's major emphases, which is the great reversal the kingdom brings. His list of beatitudes and woes are exact opposites. Jesus turns everything upside down to make an important point: the kingdom of God is the ultimate good.

### Love of One's Enemies (vv. 27–36)

Love is the heart of Jesus' teachings, and these verses are crucial to understanding what He meant. Jesus defined love as action, not emotion. Whatever we feel about our enemies, we are to act for good on their behalf.

### The Golden Rule (v. 31)

This rule sums up Jesus' main point. Notice that Jesus stated the rule positively, not negatively. The Golden Rule calls on followers of Jesus to take the initiative. How do you want others to treat you? Treat them as you want to be treated. Do the good for them that you want done for you.

The Golden Rule is also stated in Matthew 7:12. The designation, *Golden Rule*, doesn't appear in the Bible; and its origin in English is difficult to trace. The principle of the Golden Rule is found in many religions; but Jesus' wording of it was original and unique.

### Judging Others (vv. 37–42)

There is nothing unusual or difficult about liking people who like us, or doing good to those who do good to us. This is how most people act.

Jesus calls us to God's kind of love. Those who practice this kind of love are recognized as sons of God.

### Tests of Goodness (vv. 43–49)

*The Fruit Test (vv. 43–45).* A person's character is revealed by what he or she says and does. Trees are known by their fruits. Likewise, good people or evil people reveal their inner attitudes and values by their actions and words.

*The Obedience Test (vv. 46–49).* Those who call Jesus "Lord" are not really His unless they practice what He tells them to do. What they profess should match what they practice.

■ *Luke's emphasis on love for one's enemies is*
■ *seen most clearly when one compares his*
■ *expanded account with the parallel in Mat-*
■ *thew.*

## QUESTIONS TO GUIDE YOUR STUDY

1. What sparked confrontation between Jesus and the religious leaders?
2. What does it mean to be "blessed"? How do poverty, hunger, and distress transform into blessing?
3. The Golden Rule is a commonly used teaching today. What is the point of the Golden Rule?

## JESUS HEALS THE CENTURION'S SERVANT (7:1–10)

Jesus responded to the faith of a Roman centurion by healing his servant. Similar accounts are also found in Matt. 8:5–13 and John 4:46–53.

Jesus marvelled at the faith of this Gentile—a faith greater than He had found in all of Israel.

## JESUS RAISES THE WIDOW OF NAIN'S SON (7:11–17)

Part of Jesus' ministry involved restoring the dead to life.

Jesus restored the son of a widow at Nain. This young man was her only son. She was dependent on him for support, protection, and companionship. Those who witnessed this miracle were "filled with awe and praised God."

■ *In this section we find Jesus responding to*
■ *people in various ways. He was amazed at*
■ *the faith of the centurion and healed his ser-*
■ *vant. In another account, He responded with*
■ *compassion to the needs of the widow and*
■ *then brought her son back to life.*

## JESUS REVEALS HIMSELF TO JOHN THE BAPTIST (7:18–30)

### A Question (vv. 18–20)

John the Baptist had been imprisoned because he had been boldly speaking the truth. While John was in prison, his disciples brought him word of what Jesus was doing. John then sent

A centurion was a Roman officer who commanded about one hundred men. We get a uniformly favorable impressions of centurions that are mentioned in the New Testament. Centurions were usually career soldiers, and they formed the backbone of the Roman military force.

The Gospels record three specific instances of Jesus restoring the dead: (1) Jairus's daughter (Matt. 9:18–26; Mark 5:21–43; Luke 8:40–56); (2) the son of the widow of Nain (Luke 7:11), and (3) Lazarus (John 11:1–44). These people were restored to life, but later they died. Jesus' power over death in their lives, however, points to His own unique resurrection. He was raised as the conqueror of death, never again to die (Rom. 6:9).

In an account that parallels the New Testament closely, the Jewish historian, Josephus, stated that Herod Antipas arrested John and subsequently executed him at Macharaeus because "he feared that John's so extensive influence over people might lead to an uprising."

two disciples to Jesus with this question, "Are you the one who was to come, or should we expect someone else?"

### An Answer (vv. 21–23)

John's earlier statements show that he thought of the Messiah's work primarily in terms of judgment on evil. John apparently was perplexed because Jesus was not acting as he had expected.

Jesus' answer to John supports this interpretation of John's perplexity. Jesus continued His ministry of helping and healing in the presence of John's disciples. Then He sent them back with this answer to John's question: "Go back and tell John what you have seen and heard: The blind receive sight, the lame walk, those who have leprosy are cured, the deaf hear, the dead are raised, and the good news is preached to the poor."

### Jesus Bears Witness to John the Baptist as His Forerunner (vv. 24–30)

After the messengers of John left, Jesus delivered a powerful and lyrical tribute to John. He portrayed John as a bold, courageous prophet.

What Jesus told John shows that Jesus' work was a fulfillment of a number of prophesies in Isaiah: "And on that day the deaf shall hear words of a book, and out of their gloom and darkness the eyes of the blind shall see. The afflicted also shall increase their gladness in the Lord, and the needy of mankind shall rejoice in the Holy One of Israel" (Isa. 29:19).

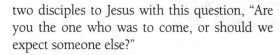

- *When John the Baptist questioned whether*
- *Jesus was really the Messiah, Jesus provided*
- *an answer which highlighted six of His*
- *works that fulfilled Old Testament messianic*
- *promises. Jesus clearly bore witness that*
- *John the Baptist was His forerunner.*

## JESUS EXPERIENCES REJECTION (7:31–35)

Some accused Jesus of the sins of the people whom He associated with. Although they rejected the austere John and his message, they also rejected the sociable Jesus and His message. In spite of the differences between John and Jesus, their message was the same.

## JESUS FORGIVES SINS (7:36–50)

Just as Jesus sometimes ate with tax collectors and sinners, so He sometimes ate with Pharisees. Therefore, when Simon the Pharisee invited Jesus to dinner, Jesus accepted.

It was not uncommon for people from the street to come in and observe such festivities. But Simon was shocked to see a sinful woman come in and proceed to anoint Jesus' feet as described in verse 38.

Simon quickly formed his own conclusion based on what he saw. He assumed two things about a prophet: (1) a prophet would have special insight into a person's character; and (2) a prophet would not knowingly let an immoral woman anoint his feet. He, therefore, concluded that Jesus was not a prophet.

To show His true prophetic insight by reading the thoughts of Simon, Jesus told the parable of the two debtors. The debtors owed a debt they could not pay. The creditor forgave them both. Each should have been grateful. Differences between what each was forgiven are relative. Each should have been grateful based on what he had been forgiven, not based on comparing his debt with the debts of others.

In response to this woman's act of worship, Jesus claimed to forgive her sins: "Your faith has

**"Sinners"**

The character of this woman is important due to Luke 7:39, 47. This woman could have been a sinner because of her occupation. Tax collectors, tanners, camel drivers, and custom collectors, among others, were considered ceremonially impure because of their occupations and could be labeled "sinners." In this instance, however, this woman's sinfulness involved moral, not ceremonial, matters.

The point of Jesus' parable is that with regard to forgiveness of sins, each of us has been forgiven a debt none of us could pay. The degree of our love and gratitude depends on our own estimate of the amount of that debt and of the grace of God in forgiving us. A person, therefore, does not have to be a sinful reprobate in order to appreciate the love of God.

saved you; go in peace." Notice that Jesus did not say, "God forgives you." Instead, He exercised His divine prerogative and personally announced that her sins were forgiven. This claim once again irritated His critics.

■ *We see Luke's theme of the great reversal in*
■ *this passage. Once again the one expected to*
■ *have the inside track to forgiveness and sal-*
■ *vation—a religious leader—is found outside*
■ *of God's kingdom. On the other hand, the*
■ *outcast—a woman who was a sinner and*
■ *despised by religious leaders such as*
■ *Simon—found forgiveness. Again the last*
■ *have become the first and the first last.*

## QUESTIONS TO GUIDE YOUR STUDY

1. What prompted John to question Jesus' messiahship? What was significant about Jesus' response to John?

2. The same people who rejected John's message also rejected Jesus' message. What about this message caused the people to reject it?

3. What was the point of Jesus' parable of the two debtors?

## LUKE 8

### A SUMMARY OF JESUS' MINISTRY (8:1–3)

At this point in his narrative, Luke summarizes Jesus' ministry of proclaiming the good news of the gospel of God's kingdom and ministry of healing. This summary is similar to that in 4:40–44, but here Luke mentions the Twelve and "some women" and even names the latter three—Mary Magdalene, Joanna, and Susanna. These women had been healed of evil spirits and other infirmities.

## THE PARABLE OF THE SOILS (8:4–15)

Jesus told the parable of four kinds of soils. They are as follows:

*Hard ground.* As in the case of the sower's seed, some of Jesus' words fell on hard ground. These people included His enemies who had closed their eyes to the light and their ears to the truth.

*Shallow soil.* Some seed fell on shallow soil; and some of Jesus' words were heard by superficial followers, whose early enthusiasm faded and disappeared in times of trouble.

*Weed-filled soil.* Still other seed fell in the weed-filled corners of the field. Some of Jesus' words gained a sympathetic hearing but never bore fruit because the hearers allowed cares and pleasures to predominate.

*Good soil.* Fortunately, some seed fell on good soil and yielded much fruit, and some of His words were heard by genuine followers whose lives testified to the reality of their faith.

## PARABLE OF THE LAMP (8:16–18)

These three verses are found elsewhere in Luke in three separate places (11:33; 12:2; 19:26). Luke uses them here to reinforce the message of the parable of the soils. Those who have heard the word with faith and commitment have the light, and the light is for sharing that others may see. God intends that the light be seen, not hidden. Each person, therefore, should be careful to hear as God intends. Hearing involves a

Luke 8:1–3 signified the higher plane to which Jesus lifted women. In His day, it was a man's world. Only males participated fully in synagogue services. Jesus treated women as persons in their own right. He not only liberated them from what afflicted them but also included them among His followers. The latter relationship was reciprocal; it included not only His help for them but also the help they could give to Him and the others.

Lesson: Response is determined by the kind of soil on which the word of the gospel falls. The seed of truth will grow only in "receptive" soil.

As followers of Christ, we must let the seed of God's Word take root in our lives so we will bear fruit.

Mark's account of this incident reveals that Jesus' family had come to try to take Him home because they thought He was losing His mind. This is understandable, for John 7:5 states that His brothers did not believe in Him. Jesus was everything a brother and a son should be, but when family interests threatened His mission, He put the will of His Father first.

two-fold responsibility—to receive and share the light.

## JESUS' TRUE FAMILY (8:19–21)

This incident further reinforced the lesson about hearing. Jesus taught here that the members of His larger family are those who hear the Word of God and do it. The occasion for this lesson was the coming of Jesus' mother and brothers.

■ *This section of Luke's narrative concerns*
■ *Jesus' teaching about the hearing of God's*
■ *Word and, in particular, hearing God's*
■ *Word in Jesus' parables. Luke informs his*
■ *readers that belonging to Jesus' family is not*
■ *a matter of physical kinship but of hearing*
■ *and doing God's Word.*

## JESUS CALMS THE SEA (8:22–25)

As the disciples were crossing the Sea of Galilee, Jesus fell asleep in the boat. Suddenly, a squall descended upon the sea. The winds and raging waters placed the boat in great danger. Fearing for their lives, the disciples awakened Jesus who got up and commanded the elements to stop.

"Where is your faith?" was Jesus' rebuke of His disciples for their lack of faith. They failed to trust God to watch them as they went about doing His will.

The disciples' fear of the storm was replaced with a different fear. After Jesus' demonstration of power, they felt fear and amazement in the presence of one who could command obedience from the winds and water: "Who is this?"

Miracle Stories in the Gospels

Jesus' calming of the sea is a typical account of a miracle story. These stories normally contain three elements:

1.a description of the need (e.g., 8:23: "they were in great danger");

2.the miracle itself (e.g., 8:24: "He...rebuked the wind and raging waters)...and all was calm."); and

3.the reaction to the miracle (e.g., 8:25: "Who is this?").

## JESUS HEALS A DEMON-POSSESSED MAN (8:26–39)

Next, Jesus and His disciples encountered a demon-possessed man. Society had tried to restrain him in chains, but he had broken these and was living among the tombs.

Jesus exorcised the demons and allowed them to enter a nearby herd of pigs.

The sad part of this story was the reaction of the people. They asked Jesus to leave. Luke mentioned their great fear as the reason. This kind of superstitious fear rejects Jesus and the help He offers.

The man healed of the demons begged Jesus to let him accompany Him. Jesus told the man to return home and tell others what God had done. This man, probably a Gentile, became the first witness for Jesus in Gentile territory.

Although God does not always shield us from the destructiveness of all life's storms, He can always be trusted to be there in the storm with us.

In this case, likely Luke wanted his readers to understand how Jesus' power and might related to their own situation. He wanted them to recognize that because of their Lord's power there was no need to fear. Jesus' power was greater than their needs. Therefore, they should not doubt or fear but only believe, for their Lord can and will calm the storms that rage against them.

## JESUS HEALS THE HEMORRHAGING WOMAN (8:40–48)

When Jesus returned to Galilee, He found the crowds waiting. As He pressed through the crowd, a woman who had been ill for twelve years with an incurable malady touched His garment, believing that doing so would heal her. Upon touching His garment, she was immediately healed. Jesus responded to her by saying, "Your faith has healed you."

## JESUS RAISES JAIRUS'S DAUGHTER (8:49–56)

While Jesus was still speaking, Jairus, the synagogue leader, received word that his daughter had died. Hearing this news, Jesus said to him, "Don't be afraid; just believe, and she will be healed." Jesus went to Jairus's house and commanded the child to "get up!" Her spirit returned to her, and she stood up.

- *These four miracles of Jesus show God's*
- *grace and power in four areas that threaten*
- *human life and welfare: (1) nature's some-*
- *times destructive force; (2) the enslavement*
- *resulting from the power of evil; (3) the pain*
- *and helplessness of lingering illness; and (4)*
- *the fearful reality of bereavement and death.*

## QUESTIONS TO GUIDE YOUR STUDY

1. What is the point of the parable of the soils? What kind of soil are you?
2. What do the four miracles of 8:22–56 tell us about Jesus?
3. What point was Luke making for his readers in his accounts of the healing of the woman with a hemorrhage and the raising of Jairus's daughter?

# LUKE 9

### THE MISSION OF THE TWELVE (9:1–6)

The disciples had been with Jesus during much of His Galilean ministry. Now Jesus sent them out to do what they had seen Him do.

### HEROD'S QUESTION ABOUT JESUS (9:7–9)

Herod Antipas heard reports of what Jesus and the Twelve were doing. He was aware of three explanations about who Jesus was: (1) some thought Jesus was John the Baptist who had been raised from the dead; (2) others thought

He was Elijah; and (3) still others believed that one of the ancient prophets had been brought back from the dead.

The report that perplexed Herod was the one about John the Baptist, whom Herod had ordered beheaded. Perhaps there was a certain amount of guilt in Herod's heart. Luke records that Herod wanted to see Jesus, perhaps to reassure himself that Jesus was not John. Luke 23:6–12 records the sad scene when Jesus and Herod finally met.

## THE FEEDING OF THE FIVE THOUSAND (9:10–17)

This miracle is the only one in all four Gospels that occurred in Galilee, and one of the few miracles recorded in all four.

After the Twelve returned from their mission, they reported to Jesus. He and the Twelve withdrew to what Luke calls "a remote place." However, the crowds heard of it and followed.

Although the disciples wanted to dismiss the crowd, Jesus commanded them to feed the crowd. The crowd numbered about five thousand and the disciples had only five loaves of bread and two fish. Taking the loaves, Jesus gave thanks and then broke the bread. He performed a miraculous multiplication of the available food and provided an abundance that was more than enough nourishment for the crowd. Luke records that the disciples gathered twelve basketfuls of leftovers.

"Disciple"

The basic meaning of the word *disciple* is "learner" or "pupil." Normally, it referred to the adherent of a particular teacher or religious/ philosophical school. Disciples of the rabbis could select their teachers. Jesus often demanded extreme levels of personal renunciation (loss of family, property, etc.). He asked for lifelong allegiance as the essential means of doing the will of God.

■ *The feeding of the five thousand was a turning point in Jesus' ministry. After this event,*

- ■ *His popularity with the masses declined, and*
- ■ *He devoted more of His time to instructing*
- ■ *the disciples.*

### PETER'S CONFESSION (9:18–22)

Each of the synoptic Gospels records the confession of Peter (Matt. 16:13–33; Mark 8:27–33), but only Luke places it in the context of Jesus' prayer life.

Peter declared Jesus to be God's promised Messiah. His confession that Jesus is "the Christ of God" is significant at this point in Luke's Gospel.

At this stage of their understanding, however, the disciples saw Jesus as the Messiah of popular Jewish expectations.

### JESUS' TEACHING ON THE PASSION AND DISCIPLESHIP (9:23–27)

Jesus explained that He would be crucified and that those who follow Him would have to take up their cross.

The word *transfigured*, in more common English, is translated "transformed." The Greek word used is *metamorphoo*, from which we get the English word *metamorphosis*.

### THE TRANSFIGURATION (9:28–36)

Each of the synoptic Gospels records the Transfiguration, but only Luke tells us that it took place while Jesus was praying.

Jesus took the three inner-circle disciples (Peter, James, and John) with Him to a high mountain, likely Mount Hermon. There they witnessed Jesus transfigured before their eyes. For that brief moment, they observed Him as the heavenly Lord. His personal appearance and that of His garments changed.

Joining Jesus and the disciples were Moses and Elijah. Luke is the only one who records what Moses, Elijah, and Jesus spoke about: "His departure, which he was about to bring to fulfillment at Jerusalem." A cloud enveloped the group, and a voice came from the cloud challenging Peter, James, and John to listen to Jesus when He told them about what the future held.

■ *The transfiguration was an open display for*
■ *the disciples of the glory Jesus had before the*
■ *Incarnation. It was also a foreshadowing of*
■ *Jesus' resurrection and return.*

## THE HEALING OF THE BOY WITH AN UNCLEAN SPIRIT (9:37–43*a*)

After Jesus and the disciples descended the mountain, they met the crowds—and a desperate situation. The disciples had been unable to heal a boy with an evil spirit.

In bringing deliverance, Jesus challenged both the father and the disciples to greater faith and ardent prayer. The father's confession of the emptiness of his faith made contact with the riches of Christ's grace. Jesus' healing of the boy left the people astonished.

## THE SECOND PASSION ANNOUNCEMENT (9:43*b*–45)

Jesus spoke again to His disciples about what lay ahead for Him. Jesus' second prediction of His passion reminded the disciples that He was a suffering Messiah rather than a conquering Messiah. They still did not grasp what He was saying.

## WHAT MAKES A PERSON GREAT? (9:46–50)

Jesus now presented instructions about discipleship and humility in order to spotlight the self-seeking strife erupting among the disciples.

In the transfiguration, Moses symbolizes the law, while Elijah stands for the prophets. Jesus had come to fulfill both. In Old Testament writings, these two men were also connected with the age of the Messiah. Their appearance with Jesus meant in part that He was the prophet Moses foretold (Deut. 18:15) and the Messiah whom Elijah would precede (Mal. 4:5).

■ *The disciples were arguing about who among*
■ *them was the greatest. Jesus used this as an*
■ *opportunity to teach them about the way of*
■ *the cross. A humble, childlike trust and a tol-*
■ *erant spirit toward others are the marks of*
■ *followers of Jesus.*

James and John were called *Boanerges*, which means "sons of thunder." The name may be indicative of the thunderous temperament these brothers apparently possessed. It is interesting to note that James would be the first apostle to give his life in the service of Christ. John would later be called the "apostle of love."

### THE MISSION TO SAMARIA (9:51–56)

This is the first mention of the Samaritans in Luke's Gospel. The people of a Samaritan village refused to welcome Jesus because He was a Jew on His way to Jerusalem. The response of James and John in verse 54 shows how far they were from sharing Jesus' commitment to the way of the cross. Wanting to call down fire on those who had rejected them is an understandable reaction, but Jesus rebuked them.

### TEACHINGS ON DISCIPLESHIP (9:57–62)

Luke has the most complete account of Jesus' contact with three prospective disciples who lacked commitment.

■ *Discipleship is not a frivolous decision. Jesus*
■ *demands unqualified commitment of His dis-*
■ *ciples. Those who will be His disciples must*
■ *first count the cost before making such a*
■ *commitment.*

### QUESTIONS TO GUIDE YOUR STUDY

1. What lessons did the feeding of the five thousand teach the disciples? What does this event teach us about Jesus?
2. Review the Gospel accounts of the Transfiguration (Matt. 16:27–17:8; Mark

8:38–9:8; Luke 9:26–36). What was its purpose? Why were Elijah and Moses present?

3. What was the disciples' understanding of Jesus' messiahship? Why was Peter's confession significant?

## LUKE 10

### THE TRAINING OF THE SEVENTY FOR MISSIONARY SERVICE (10:1–16)

At this point Luke records the mission of the seventy, which is similar to the mission of the Twelve in 9:1–6. Luke provides more fully Jesus' instruction here than he did for the earlier sending of the Twelve.

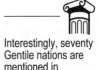

Interestingly, seventy Gentile nations are mentioned in Genesis 10.

■ *Jesus appointed seventy missionaries who*
■ *were to go ahead of Him to every town and*
■ *place He was about to go. They were "sent*
■ *ones" who would proclaim the gospel mes-*
■ *sage and prepare the villages for Jesus' spiri-*
■ *tual coming and resurrection.*

### CAUSE FOR REJOICING (10:17–24)

#### The Return of the Seventy (vv. 17–20)

The words *joy* and *rejoice* are the keys to this passage The seventy returned with joy after their successful mission. Jesus shared their joy but reminded them to rejoice primarily not in being empowered for service but in having been saved by grace.

**Samaria and Samaritans**

In the days of Christ, the relationship between the Jews and the Samaritans was greatly strained. The animosity was so great that the Jews bypassed Samaria as they traveled between Galilee and Judea. They went an extra distance through the barren land of Perea on the eastern side of the Jordan River to avoid going through Samaria. Jesus forbade this animosity. He rebuked His disciples for their hostility to the Samaritans (Luke 9:55–56), healed a Samaritan leper (Luke 17:16), honored a Samaritan for his neighborliness (Luke 10:30–37), praised a Samaritan for his gratitude (Luke 17:11–18), asked a drink of a Samaritan woman (John 4:7), and preached to the Samaritans. Then in Acts 1:8, Jesus challenged His disciples to witness in Samaria. Philip, a deacon, opened a mission in Samaria (Acts 8:5). A small Samaritan community continues to this day to follow the traditional worship near Shechem.

*The Blessedness of the Disciples (vv. 21–24)*

These verses complete the description of the responsibilities and privileges of discipleship begun in 9:51.

- *The seventy who were appointed and sent to*
- *proclaim the gospel returned rejoicing over a*
- *successful mission. Jesus told them that they*
- *had been privileged to see and hear what the*
- *kings and prophets of the old order had*
- *yearned to see and hear.*

## THE PARABLE OF THE GOOD SAMARITAN (10:25–37)

A lawyer asked Jesus two questions. The first question was, "What must I do to inherit eternal life?" Jesus responded by telling the lawyer the answer was written in the law. The lawyer correctly identified Deut. 6:5 and Lev. 19:18 as the answer. This led to the second question, "And who is my neighbor?" Jesus answered with the parable of the Good Samaritan. This parable is unique to Luke and does not appear to be linked chronologically to the preceding or following incidents. Probably no parable has been allegorized more often than this one.

On the road between Jerusalem and Jericho, a Jewish traveler was assaulted by violent men, who robbed him and left him for dead. Both a priest and a Levite who passed by refused to help their injured countryman because they would incur expensive and inconvenient ceremonial defilement by contact with someone who might be dead. Jesus shocked His audience by suddenly introducing a hated Samaritan who showed compassion by dressing the victim's wounds, letting the man ride the donkey through dangerous territory while he walked, and paying money to an innkeeper for an extended convalescence for the injured man. The Samaritan even promised credit for the additional funds if they were needed.

■ *The Samaritan showed by his actions what*
■ *love is. The reality of his compassion is seen*
■ *in what he did to help the man. Christian*
■ *love is acting for the good of the other per-*
■ *sons—whoever they are, whatever the cost,*
■ *and however we feel.*

The seventeen-mile road from Jerusalem to Jericho drops more than one thousand feet. It is wild country with many places for robbers to hide.

## MARTHA AND MARY (10:38–42)

Luke alone records this incident. The story emphasizes that quiet dependence on Jesus is more important than bustling service.

■ *Within this short passage is a clear empha-*
■ *sis on the importance of hearing Jesus' word.*
■ *To listen to Jesus as Mary did is the best*
■ *thing one can do, even better than serving.*

Jesus deliberately chose an outsider, and a hated one at that, for His hero in order to indicate that being a neighbor is not a matter of nationality or race. He used the parable to show the lawyer that he had asked the wrong question. The question should not be, "Who is my neighbor?" but "To whom can I be a neighbor?"

## QUESTIONS TO GUIDE YOUR STUDY

1. Why does Luke provide such a strong emphasis on the mission of the seventy?

2. Describe the mission of the seventy. Were they successful? How were the seventy "blessed"?

3. Contrast the attitudes of Mary and Martha. What was Jesus' response to each?

Disciples of the rabbis often asked for instruction on specific practices. In view of all the disciples had seen Jesus do, it is interesting that they asked Him to teach them to pray.

## JESUS' TEACHING ON PRAYER (11:1–13)

### The Model Prayer (vv. 1–4)

Luke's Gospel emphasizes Jesus' prayer life. The disciples' awareness of this caused them to make their request. He answered them first by giving them a model prayer.

The prayer includes several petitions.

*"Hallowed be your name."* This first petition asks God to cause His name to be hallowed or "glorified." "Name" refers to God's reputation and thus His honor.

*"Your kingdom come."* Although the kingdom had already come in Jesus' ministry, its final consummation will be in the future.

*"Give us this day our daily bread."* There is confusion about what the word *daily* means. Suggested meanings are: 1) bread that is essential for existence, 2) bread of the coming day or, 3) bread for the present day.

*"Forgive us our sins."* The Model Prayer assumes the regular need for confessing of sin, even as 1 John 1:9 does. The issue is not one of salvation, but the regular cleansing from sin that each believer needs.

*"Lead us not into temptation."* Helpful paraphrases of this idea might include, "Do not allow us to enter into temptation that could destroy us" or "Keep us from yielding to temptation."

"Bread" is an example of a figure of speech known as *synecdoche*, in which a part (bread) represents the whole (food). Bread, therefore, is a request for the basic necessities of life, not for luxuries.

■ *The Model Prayer contains the components*
■ *and attitudes that Jesus' disciples should*
■ *exhibit and incorporate into their lives. The*
■ *first half of this prayer focuses God-ward*
■ *while the second half focuses us-ward. It's an*
■ *example of the kind of prayer God hears*
■ *and honors.*

### The Need to Pray (vv. 5–8)

After teaching the disciples how to pray, Jesus turned to a more difficult task—to teach them the *need* to pray. Jesus reinforced the Model Prayer with the parable of the persistent friend.

### The Encouragement to Pray (vv. 9–13)

Verse 9 is an encouragement to continue in praying, whereas verse 10 is a promise to those who do.

The progression of commands—ask, seek, knock—is an example of the figure of speech called *synonymous parallelism*, in which the same basic thought is repeated rhythmically.

■ *The person who prays out of a sense of need*
■ *is the one who truly learns to pray.*

### THE BEELZEBUB CONTROVERSY (11:14–23)

Beelzebub is the name used for Satan in the New Testament. On more than one occasion, Jesus' opponents accused Him of being linked with the devil. Here He answered them by using language reminiscent of Exod. 8:19 to point to the irresistible conclusion that God's power was at

We learn to pray by praying. The one who prays out of a sense of need is the one who truly learns to pray. Jesus insisted that perseverance with a God-honored request will bring a positive result. It is important to keep in mind that the context makes clear that our persistence does not pressure a reluctant God into responding to our requests; rather, He examines our motives to determine the presence of genuine desire.

"Then the magicians said to Pharaoh, 'This is the finger of God.' But Pharaoh's heart was hardened and he did not listen to them, as the LORD had said" (Exod. 8:19, NASB).

work. God was using the casting out of demons to press His sovereign claims on those who saw these signs.

## THE RETURN OF THE UNCLEAN SPIRIT AND TRUE BLESSEDNESS (11:24–28)

Jesus' concluding warning shows that a person who expelled the spirit of evil (that is, a demon) must replace it with a more powerful source of strength. The kingdom of God can bring a full and complete victory over evil.

## THE SIGN OF JONAH (11:29–32)

At this point, Luke answers the request for a sign in 11:16 by linking it to the tradition concerning the present generation's desire for a sign.

Signs do not produce faith. Even the greatest sign, the Resurrection, will not produce faith in an unwilling heart.

## SAYINGS ABOUT LIGHT (11:33–36)

A lamp is made to shine. The eye is like a lamp for the body: good eyes illumine, but diseased eyes distort and darken.

## A DENUNCIATION OF THE PHARISEES AND SCRIBES (11:37–54)

After Jesus spoke, He accepted an invitation from a Pharisee to have lunch. When Jesus failed to follow rabbinic tradition for hand washing before eating, His host was astonished. Jesus sensed his host's displeasure and warned the Pharisee of the danger of emphasizing the external over the internal. What follows is a series of six woes: three against the Pharisees (vv. 42–44) and three against the lawyers or scribes (vv. 42–52).

**"Woe"**

The word *woe* is an interjection of grief or denunciation and is often rendered "alas!" Jesus used the word *woe* here not as a curse but as an expression of deep regret. Jesus' purpose for these woes was to expose the sins of the Pharisees and lawyers to try to help them and the people adversely influenced by them.

■ With a series of woes, Jesus strongly
■ denounced the Pharisees' and lawyers' prac-
■ tices that emphasized the outward over the
■ inward, thus allowing their hypocrisy to
■ remain unchanged.

## QUESTIONS TO GUIDE YOUR STUDY

1. What encouragements to pray does Jesus give us?

2. What was the sign of Jonah? Why did Jesus give the people this sign?

3. Why did Jesus denounce the Pharisees and lawyers? How relevant are Jesus' woes when applied to today's religious systems?

## LUKE 12 ---------------------

This chapter consists primarily of teachings Jesus addressed to His followers. The chapter's three main themes are 1) courageous confession, 2) the proper perspective on possessions; and 3) faithful stewardship.

## WARNINGS AND EXHORTATIONS (12:1–12)

### Beware Hypocrisy (vv. 1–3)

Hypocrites try to hide the truth by pretending to be something they are not. Jesus charged the Pharisees with hypocrisy because they tried to hide what they really were behind masks of outward religious practices.

"All kinds of greed"

Greed is an insatiable desire and lust for more and more. It is all-consuming, so that all of life becomes focused on the accumulation of wealth. There is no room for anything, not even God. This is why it is so hard for a rich person to enter God's kingdom.

This uncontrolled behavior very often is the reason for damaged or destroyed relationships as it is a grasping after the most and the best without regard for others.

"By the fear of the Lord, men depart from evil; by the fear of man, they run themselves into evil."

John Flavel

The Unpardonable Sin

The unpardonable sin involves setting one's mind against the Holy Spirit and crediting Satan with what is God's work. To do this is to blaspheme against the Holy Spirit. To "blaspheme" means to speak an insult against someone so as to defame a person's reputation and character.

The unpardonable sin is not restricted to Jesus' day. It happens today when a person sees a work that is without question God's work, but claims it is Satan's work.

### Fear and Trust (vv. 4–7)

Verses 4–12 clearly refer to a persecution situation. In such a time, disciples will be tempted to fear their persecutors. Why should they fear when all that persecutors can do is kill them? The Bible consistently declares that the fear of God is the only fear that is justified. If people fear God, they need be afraid of nothing else.

### Speaking Up for Christ (vv. 8–12)

In situations when believers are tempted to deny Christ, they must be on their guard against denying Him in word or deed.

This passage does warn about a sin for which there is no forgiveness. The person who persists in rejecting light and truth stands in danger of becoming so hardened that he or she attributes the work of the Spirit to Satan (cp. Matt. 12:24–32). This is more than a personal affront against Jesus; it is a hardening of the heart against every attempt by God's Spirit to bring mercy, grace, and truth. Only people who refuse forgiveness are unforgivable.

■ *Having denounced (with the six woes) the*
■ *glaring inconsistency of the Pharisees'*
■ *behavior, Jesus' warning against their*
■ *hypocrisy makes a fitting conclusion. Jesus*
■ *also warns believers about fear, confession,*
■ *and the unpardonable sin, but He assures*
■ *them of God's presence and the Spirit's guid-*
■ *ance in times of persecution.*

### THE PARABLE OF THE RICH FOOL (12:13–21)

Jesus refused to act as a judge in a family dispute about inheritance. He chose instead to deal with the moral issue involved in the dispute: covetousness. *Covetousness* is a combination of greed and envy. It is the desire for more and more, which often is activated by wanting what someone else has.

- *The parable of the rich fool is about greed*
- *and the folly of one's reliance on wealth.*
- *Jesus warned His followers against all forms*
- *of greed.*

## CARE AND ANXIETY (12:22–34)

Having given a negative example of the principle in verse 15 with the parable of the rich fool, Luke provides a corrective to the believer's relationship to possessions. Whereas covetousness is the desire for more and more but never getting enough, anxiety is the crippling fear that there may not be enough.

The catchword in this section is *worry*. Jesus told His disciples that they need not worry for daily bread or clothing. In His sovereign care of His creation, God feeds the ravens and clothes the lilies. How much more, then, will He care for His children.

"The lilies Jesus spoke of were the scarlet anemones. After one of the infrequent showers of summer rain, the mountain side would be scarlet with them; they bloomed one day and died"

William Barclay, *The Gospel of Luke*, 165.

- *If all of nature trusts God to meet its needs,*
- *God's children should trust Him to meet their*
- *needs. Rather than worry about "things" or*
- *use them as substitutes for life, believers*
- *should concentrate on the concerns of*
- *the kingdom.*

## THE WATCHFUL SERVANTS (12:35–48)

Whereas stewardship of possessions is implicit in the previous section, the rest of this chapter deals with stewardship of life and service. It does so in connection with the Lord's coming. The three parables on vigilance that follow emphasize the need for His followers to be ready for His coming.

## JESUS—THE GREAT DIVIDER (12:49–53)

Jesus saw that the outcome of His mission would be a crisis out of which would come judgment and division. Jesus had come to bring peace. His ultimate intent is not to bring the kind of division described in verses 51–53, but such division is inevitable when some choose to follow Christ and others reject Him.

## SIGNS OF THE TIME AND SETTLING WITH ONE'S OPPONENTS (12:54–59)

The multitudes to which Jesus spoke had an amazing lack of awareness of what was going on around them. They could read nature's signs, but they did not read the signs of the times in which they lived.

■ *As believers, we must see that nothing keeps*
■ *us from serving God faithfully, whether it be*
■ *the seeming delay of Jesus' coming, persecu-*
■ *tion, or the unbelieving attitude of the world.*

## QUESTIONS TO GUIDE YOUR STUDY

1. What was the nature of the Pharisees' hypocrisy? What was sinful about it?

2. What is the unpardonable sin? Why is it unforgivable?

3. What is the relationship between our stewardship of life and service and the Lord's coming? What should be the believer's stance regarding His return?

# LUKE 13  - - - - - - - - - - - - - - - - - - - - - -

## THE NEED TO REPENT (13:1–9)

### *Lessons from Tragedy (vv. 1–5)*

The controversy story (vv. 1–5) and parable (vv. 6–9) in this passage are unique to Luke's Gospel. Verses 1–3 refer to a recent incident in which Pontius Pilate had a number of Galileans killed while they were offering sacrifices in the Temple. Verses 4–5 recount another tragedy, the collapse of the Tower of Siloam, which killed eighteen residents of Jerusalem.

The self-righteousness of reporters of the incident at the Temple assumed the Galileans got what they deserved. Also, many assumed the construction accident at the tower was a divine judgment on workers willing to be paid with divine money. Jesus points out that in both incidents the victims of these tragedies were not especially evil. The lesson Jesus drew from these examples was the audience's need to repent.

### *Parable of the Barren Fig Tree (vv. 6–9)*

This parable complements the teaching in verses 1–5. A tree that had received special treatment from its owner had not borne fruit. The owner of the fig tree had every right to expect fruit after three years. He ordered it cut down, not only because it was useless, but also because it exhausted the soil.

"The incident is recorded nowhere else, but is in entire harmony with Pilate's record for outrages. These Galileans at the feast in Jerusalem may have been involved in some insurrection against the Roman government, the leaders of whom Pilate had slain right in the temple courts where the sacrifices were going on. Jesus commented on the incident, but not as the reporters had expected. Instead of denunciation of Pilate He turned it into a parable for their own conduct in the uncertainty of life."

A.T. Robertson, *Word Pictures in the New Testament*, vol. 2, 185.

Although the immediate application of this entire section (Luke 12:54–13:9) was to Israel, the principles apply to persons and groups in every generation. No issue is more urgent that the need to repent; the alternative is inevitable judgment.

The vinedresser, however, interceded to give the tree one last opportunity. If the tree did not bear fruit in the coming year after additional care and treatment, it would then be cut down. The parable's point is that although God is patient and forbearing, continued refusal to repent spells certain doom.

■ Jesus' main lesson to His audience was the
■ need to repent while there is opportunity.

### THE HEALING OF THE CRIPPLED WOMAN ON THE SABBATH (13:10–17)

The debate over the proper use of the Sabbath caused continuing controversy between Jesus and His opponents. Here Jesus took the initiative. He used His authority and power by healing on the Sabbath a woman who, for eighteen years, had been incapable of walking erectly. The action annoyed the synagogue leader, who said to the crowd, "There are six days for work. So come and be healed on those days, not on the Sabbath."

Jesus denounced the leader's hypocrisy by showing that Jewish legalists violated the Sabbath in feeding their animals. The result was that while the people rejoiced in this display of God's glory and power, the ruler and Jesus' other adversaries were humiliated.

### THE PARABLES OF THE MUSTARD SEED AND LEAVEN (13:18–21)

#### The Mustard Seed (vv. 18–19)
Jesus first compared God's kingdom to what happens when a tiny mustard seed is sown. That little seed grows into a treelike plant as

high as ten feet—large enough for birds to nest in its branches.

### The Leaven (vv. 20–21)

He then compared God's kingdom to what happens when a little leaven is added to a batch of meal. Only a small amount of leaven is required to make dough rise. The increase in size brought about by leaven was one of Jesus' points.

■ *Jesus told the parables of the mustard seed*
■ *and the leaven to affirm the certainty of*
■ *God's purpose. The mustard seed grows into*
■ *a tree large enough for many nesting birds.*
■ *Even so will the kingdom's influence extend*
■ *like a tree to encompass many.*

### THE NARROW DOOR (13:22–30)

Luke begins the second part of his travel narrative by mentioning Jesus' journey toward Jerusalem. Someone from the crowd asked Jesus the question, "Lord, are only a few people going to be saved?" He did not answer the question directly. In essence, He asked another question, *Are you among the saved?*

The door of salvation stood open to any who would enter. The "many" who "will try to enter and will not be able to" are those who wait until the door is closed before trying to enter. No amount of effort or excuses will avail once the door is closed.

■ *Jesus is the one who controls the destiny of*
■ *humanity. He possesses the keys of the*

Commenting on the point of these two parables, scholar I. Howard Marshall notes, "The stress is not so much on the idea of growth in itself as on the certainty that what appears tiny and insignificant will prove to have been the beginning of a mighty kingdom"

I. Howard Marshall, *The Gospel of Luke,* (Grand Rapids: Eerdmans), 561.

**"Fox"**

Why did Jesus call Herod a "fox"? He may have referred to a fox's renowned cunning. If so, He was discounting Herod's death threat as a strategy to try to frighten Jesus away. In that day, "fox" also meant an insignificant person, as contrasted to a "lion," a person of true greatness.

- kingdom and as a result also of death and
- Hades. A person's ultimate destiny is deter-
- mined by whether Jesus will say on the final
- day, "I know you."

## WARNING ABOUT HEROD AND THE LAMENT OVER JERUSALEM (13:31–35)

We are not told why the Pharisees reported Herod's death threat to Jesus. He directed His reply to Herod; therefore, He accepted the report as accurate.

## QUESTIONS TO GUIDE YOUR STUDY

1. What is the point of the parable of the barren fig tree? How does it apply to all generations?
2. Why were the Jewish leaders of Jesus' day at odds with Him about the Sabbath?
3. What are Jesus' warnings in the "narrow door" passage (vv. 22–30)? What is the point we all need to heed?

**"Dropsy"**

Dropsy is *edema*, a disease characterized by fluid retention and swelling. Dropsy is a symptom of disease of the heart, liver, kidneys, or brain. The condition involves the accumulation of water fluid in the body cavities or in the limbs.

# LUKE 14

In this chapter Luke brought together a block of three episodes critical of the Pharisees. All three episodes center on eating, and they illustrate the hostility which official Judaism displayed toward Jesus and His gospel.

## HEALING OF THE MAN WITH DROPSY (14:1–6)

Luke highlighted the distorted values of the Pharisees, who showed no concern for the sick man. Under the guise of piety, they sought to censure Jesus for His Sabbath behavior. Jesus showed compassion for the man, healed him, and then silenced His opponents.

# SAYINGS CONCERNING BANQUET BEHAVIOR (14:7–14)

In the context of Jesus' dining with a Pharisee, Luke introduces two unique sets of ethical teachings that illustrate Christian attitudes and behavior.

## Seeking the Chief Places (vv. 7–11)

The first set of teachings is called a "parable," which is somewhat surprising, for what follows does not appear to be what is traditionally thought of as a parable. The instructions are to be taken literally, of course, but they also teach a general attitude toward self and others which is appropriate for members of God's kingdom.

## Making a Guest List (vv. 12–14)

This second set of sayings turned to the case of a host who was self-seeking in his selection of guests. Hosts were challenged not to invite guests who were able to reciprocate. One should, instead, use the banquet as an opportunity to help those who cannot reciprocate. Four groups are mentioned: the poor, the crippled, the lame, and the blind.

■ *Luke highlighted the distorted values of the*
■ *Pharisees, who showed no concern for the*
■ *sick man (14:1–6), maneuvered for status*
■ *(vv. 7–11), and lacked compassion for the*
■ *poor and needy (vv. 12–14). In contrast to*
■ *the behavior of the Pharisees, Jesus called*
■ *His hearers to display humility (v. 11) and*
■ *mercy (v. 12).*

The chief seats were the first reclining places at the table. A. T. Robertson notes, "On a couch holding three the middle place was the chief one. . . . The place next to the host on the right was then, as now, the post of honour."

A. T. Robertson, *Word Pictures in the New Tesament*, vol 2, 195

One who did this would be rewarded not by the recipients (see 16:3–7, where a steward acted with this purpose in mind), but by God at the day of judgment.

A couple of Luke's themes surface in this passage. First, he emphasized the need of humility before others and especially before God. Pride and arrogance are abominations before God. The great reversal seen here should be understood as a rejection of the proud, who exalt themselves, in favor of those who humble themselves.

## THE PARABLE OF THE GREAT BANQUET (14:15–24)

Jesus viewed God's kingdom as a joyful, sumptuous feast to which God issues a gracious invitation. Verse 16 refers to an initial invitation, whereas verse 17 refers to a later announcement when the feast is actually ready.

### Making Excuses (vv. 18–20)

In many parts of the Middle East, both then and now, to refuse a second summons was a serious breach of etiquette which could result in war.

Presumably all the guests had accepted the initial invitation; but when the slave announced the feast, they joined in what appears to be a conspiracy of excuses. The three excuses given are examples of the lame excuses given by the entire group.

### There Is Still Room (vv. 21–24)

The clear teaching of the Scriptures is that God's intent from the beginning has been to include all people in the invitation. No one is excluded except those who refuse to accept the invitation.

■ *The rejection of Jesus and the kingdom by*
■ *official Judaism precipitated the inclusion of*
■ *Israel's outcasts and the Gentiles. The great*
■ *reversal has taken place. This parable also*
■ *contains an emphasis on God's providential*
■ *rule of history. The rejection of the gospel by*
■ *Israel's leadership will not thwart God's*
■ *plan. The kingdom has come, the banquet*
■ *room will be filled, and God's plan will be*
■ *accomplished.*

# THE CONDITIONS OF DISCIPLESHIP (14:25–35)

After the parable of the great banquet, Luke relates a number of Jesus' teachings that set forth three conditions of discipleship:

*Condition #1: Hate (v. 26).* Jesus' statement in verse 26 referred to those times when family loyalty comes in conflict with one's commitment to Christ.

*Condition #2: Crossbearing (v. 27).* To bear a cross in Jesus' day meant to be willing to die a martyr's death. Jesus used this challenge earlier in calling His disciples to deny self in total commitment to Him and His way. In this context, hating one's life means a willingness to give one's life for Christ's sake.

*Condition #3: Total Commitment (vv. 28–33).* A disciple must relinquish everything.

*Hate* is "the language of exaggerated contrast, it is true, but it must not be watered down till the point is gone."

A. T. Robertson

- ■ *Salvation is free, but it is not cheap. It*
- ■ *involves repentance, commitment, and*
- ■ *renunciation of anything that stands in the*
- ■ *way of the abundant life to which Christ*
- ■ *calls His disciples.*

The coin was a drachma, representing about a day's wage for an average worker.

## QUESTIONS TO GUIDE YOUR STUDY

1. What truths is Jesus conveying with His ethical teachings about banquet behavior?

2. What is the point of the parable of the great banquet?

3. Read verse 26. When becoming a disciple of Jesus, what does it mean to hate one's family?

"Edersheim quotes a Jewish saying, 'There is joy before God when those who provoke him perish from the earth.' But Jesus has a very difference concept of God. He rejoices over the returning penitent more than over many safely in the fold."

Leon Morris, *The Gospel According to St. Luke* (Grand Rapids: Eerdmans, 1974), 238.

Luke 15 is among the most famous chapters in the Bible. The most familiar part is the story of the prodigal son.

The following three parables are connected by a theme—the joy of the lost being found.

### PARABLE OF THE LOST SHEEP (15:3–17)

The story is of a shepherd who had a hundred sheep and lost one of them. He looked for the lost sheep until he found it. Placing it on his shoulders, he brought it home. What follows is a time of rejoicing.

- ■ *This parable focuses on the shepherd's con-*
- ■ *cern for one lost sheep, his diligence in seek-*
- ■ *ing it, and his joy in finding it. Jesus teaches*
- ■ *that these are God's attitudes toward sinners.*

### PARABLE OF THE LOST COIN (15:8–10)

A woman was concerned over the loss of one coin. She diligently sought it and rejoiced when she found it. Jesus spelled out the parable's lesson: "In the same way, I tell you, there is rejoicing in the presence of the angels of God over one sinner who repents."

### PARABLE OF THE PRODIGAL SON (15:11–32)

This parable might better be titled the parable of the gracious father, for that is the true focus of its teaching.

### The Prodigal's Plight (vv. 11–16)

From a human point of view, the prodigal son can be faulted primarily for disregarding his responsibilities as a son toward his father. Insofar as his actions typify sinners, he shows the folly of misusing God-given freedom to seek freedom from a responsible relationship to God. Sinners squander God's gifts in a futile search for life and fulfillment on their own terms.

According to the Jewish principles of inheritance, the older son would receive two-thirds of the estate and the younger brother one-third.

### The Prodigal's Decision (vv. 17–19)

The previous two parables focused on the seeking love of God, but they did not show the sinner's response to that love. When a shepherd finds a lost sheep, he needs only to pick it up. The same is true of a lost coin. But a lost person is different. When a person is lost, the person must choose to receive God's forgiving love.

Jesus said that the prodigal "came to his senses." Like someone awakening from a dream, he came to grips with reality. He saw himself as he was and remembered his father's house. As yet, he felt no hope of restoration to sonship. He dared to hope only that his father would hire him as a servant. He knew his father treated his servants much better than his current employer treated him.

### The Father's Welcome (vv. 20–24)

Just as the shepherd and the woman rejoiced over finding the sheep and the coin, the father rejoiced over finding the son.

"The calf would be enough to feed the whole village; this would be a big party! Aristocratic families often invited the whole town to a banquet when a son attained adulthood (about thirteen years old) or a child married."

Craig S. Keener in *The Bible Background Commentary*, 233.

The waiting father rushed to welcome his son. Before the prodigal could finish his carefully rehearsed confession, the father gave orders to bring out the best robe for his son, to put a ring on his finger and sandals on his feet. He then called for a fatted calf to be killed and a feast to begin.

### The Older Brother's Complaints (vv. 25–30)

The older brother's complaints about the father's treatment of the prodigal match the Pharisees' complaint about Jesus' treatment of sinners.

### The Father's Entreaty (vv. 31–32)

The father's response was patient and gracious. The proud son had complained that he had been reduced to the status of a slave. If so, the father implied, this was by his own choice, not the father's. As far as the father was concerned, all the privileges of sonship were his if he would but recognize it. The father entreated his older son to share in the joy of the restoration of the younger son and brother.

At this point, Jesus left the story open-ended. The curtain fell without hearing the older son's response to this father's entreaty. These parables in this passage emphasize God's love and grace for outcasts. God accepts all repentant sinners, no matter how outcast they may be.

### QUESTIONS TO GUIDE YOUR STUDY

1. In the parable of the prodigal son, who and what do the key fictional characters represent in the real world?
2. What is the main point of the parable of the prodigal son?
3. From the three parables in this chapter, what do we learn about the character and attributes of God the Father?

The proper use of money is one of the themes of Luke's Gospel. All of chapter 16 is devoted to it.

## THE PARABLE OF THE DISHONEST MANAGER (16:1–8a)

A manager oversaw a rich man's estate. He was accused of wasting his employer's possessions. This wastefulness may have resulted from incompetence or dishonesty or both. His employer told him to turn over the records of the estate as part of giving up his position as manager.

Aware that he was soon to be unemployed, the manager began to plan for his future needs. He hit on a scheme to use his present position to make friends who would care for him when times got bad. He called his employer's debtors and, one by one, reduced their debts.

Outsiders who heard about the cancellation of the interest would have assumed the rich man authorized this action because of his religious scruples. The rich man, therefore, did not want to lose his new reputation as a man who put principle above property. It was in this spirit that the rich man commended the shrewdness of the dishonest manager.

"Shrewdly"

"Shrewdly" is a morally neutral term. Here it refers to the keen foresight with which the manager prepared himself for being fired. This adverb comes from the Greek word for "mind," the discerning intellect. Synonyms would include "discreetly" and "prudently."

"The lord does not absolve the steward from guilt and he was apparently dismissed from his service. His shrewdness consisted in finding a place to go by his shrewdness. He remained the steward of unrighteousness even though his shrewdness was commended"

A. T. Robertson, "Luke," *Word Pictures in the New Testament*, vol. 2, 217.

- Someday money and possessions will be use-
- less. However, money can be used now in
- ways that create an eternal fellowship. When
- life comes to an end, the wisdom of lasting
- investments will become clear.

## SAYINGS ON STEWARDSHIP (16:8b–18)

### *A Lesson for Sons of Light (vv. 8b–9)*

The latter half of verse 8 begins Jesus' observations about the parable. The rich man in the story commended the shrewd scoundrel, and Jesus observed that the sons of light can learn a lesson from this son of darkness. Jesus did not commend the manager's dishonesty, but He did point to the manager's initiative and foresight in planning for the future.

### *Money—The Acid Test (vv. 10–12)*

A wealthy father may entrust his son with a small amount of responsibility before the son comes of age. The son's faithfulness in a little shows he also will be faithful over all that ultimately will be entrusted to him.

### *Money—Possession or Possessor? (v. 13)*

A person can serve only one God. If a person's attitudes and actions are preoccupied with money, money becomes that person's master.

### *Contrasting Views about Money (vv. 14–15)*

When the Pharisees heard what Jesus said about money, they scoffed at Him. They viewed money differently. They saw money as evidence of God's favor, not as a false god threatening to take God's place.

### *The Danger of Self-Justification (vv. 16–18)*

The Pharisees prided themselves on their careful observation of the Law and often accused Jesus of disregarding their laws and traditions. In verse 17 Jesus affirmed the lasting importance of the moral truth in the Law. He then touched on an issue about divorce.

# THE PARABLE OF THE RICH MAN AND LAZARUS (16:19–31)

This parable is unusual in that it is the only parable in which a character is named.

When Lazarus died, he was carried away by angels. (Lazarus's name means "God has helped.") The rich man (sometimes called "Dives" from the Latin word for "rich") died and was buried, no doubt with a lavish funeral and many eloquent eulogies. However, there were no ministering angels to take him to heaven. Instead, he found himself in Hades.

The parable's lessons come in two parts. It illustrates the blessedness of the poor believer (v. 20) and the woe of the unbelieving rich (v. 24).

■ *Jesus taught that money and possessions are*
■ *gifts and trusts from God. God loans us these*
■ *with the expectation that we will use them to*
■ *help others. When we do, we are drawn*
■ *closer to God and to those who are helped.*

## QUESTIONS TO GUIDE YOUR STUDY

1. What is the point of the parable of the dishonest manager? About what was he dishonest?
2. How should the believer view money? What is the danger of placing one's trust in money?
3. What lessons do we learn from the parable of the rich man and Lazarus?

"It is clear what the rich man's sin was. He was rich, he abounded in luxuries. Scripture has not accused him of enjoying riches in iniquity, or of giving to harlots, or of being a murderer or committing any other crime. His sin was pride, the greatest of all sins; and in fulness of bread and overflowing of abundance he had not pity for the man who lay at this gate wasted by sores, but was uplifted by such pride, despising poverty, as to take not account of either the suffering of his inferiors or the common rights of humanity."

Origen

"Little ones" (v. 2) are not only children but also persons of immature faith. The bad example of a Christian, especially a Christian leader, has a disastrous impact on those who are looking for an example of what a Christian should be.

Faith that "moves mountains"

Jesus spoke of faith that can uproot a tree and plant it in the sea. Matthew's parallel involves moving a mountain from one place to another. These hyperbolic expressions describe what faith can do. But in practice, Jesus was not speaking of a faith that stages a miraculous event but of a faith that facilitates healing (Luke 7:9; 8:48; 18:42; Acts 14:9), that understands the need of Christ to suffer (Luke 24:25–26), that has confidence in God's providential care( 8:25), that will not fall away (8:13; 22:32) but will endure (Acts 14:22), and that will believe God and grow (Acts 6:5; Luke 1:45 with 1:20).

## LUKE 17

### TEACHINGS ADDRESSED TO THE DISCIPLES (17:1–10)

This is a collection of four of Jesus' sayings.

#### Beware Leading Others Astray (vv. 1–2)

Jesus warned His disciples against doing anything that would cause others to fall into sin.

#### When Your Brother Sins Against You (vv. 3–4)

The word *brother* shows the close ties that bind members of the family of faith. Verses 1–2 warn against offending a brother. And verses 3–4 tell us what to do when a brother or sister has sinned against us: "Rebuke him, and if he repents, forgive him." Verse 4 shows that no limits are to be placed on this forgiveness.

God absorbed the hurt of our sin on the cross, and offers us forgiveness and reconciliation.

#### Increase Your Faith (vv. 5–6)

The demands of discipleship are great. The disciples recognized they needed divine help to fulfill such demands. Therefore, they said to Jesus, "Increase our faith!"

Jesus' answer clarified the nature of true faith. The issue is not a need for greater faith—if by that we mean something we are capable of doing. Even faith as small as a tiny mustard seed opens the way for God to act out of His limitless resources.

#### Beware Pride (vv. 7–10)

Pride is among the greatest dangers we face as believers. Jesus used a parable to illustrate His point. The parable of the unprofitable servant is directed to the human tendency to say, "What a great person I am" rather than "How great is God!" Believers are like servants who, when they have done all that was demanded of them, can at best confess that they are unworthy and have only fulfilled their obligations.

■ *Luke provides a collection of sayings about*
■ *discipleship with respect to believers' rela-*
■ *tionships to their neighbors and their per-*
■ *sonal relationships with God.*

### THE GRATEFUL SAMARITAN (17:11–19)

This account of the grateful Samaritan begins with Jesus' healing of ten lepers at a distance. Jesus didn't touch them. He didn't even declare they were healed. He simply commanded them to go and show themselves to the priests. As they proceeded to the priests, they were healed. One of the lepers, upon observing his healing, returned to give thanks to Jesus. Luke then pointed out that this leper was a Samaritan.

■ *This healing account provides another exam-*
■ *ple of Jesus' power. Luke presents a key truth*
■ *for his readers: One can experience God's*
■ *work of grace yet fall short of receiving*
■ *salvation.*

### THE COMING OF THE KINGDOM OF GOD (17:20–37)

#### *The Kingdom Has Come (vv. 20–21)*

The time of the kingdom's coming was a subject of great interest to the Pharisees. However, their understanding of the nature of the kingdom caused them to miss its present reality. Jesus taught that the kingdom was already among them: "The kingdom of God is within you."

### The Kingdom Is Coming (vv. 22–24)

The term *kingdom*, as used by Jesus, means reign, not realm. It is the reign of God as King. God has always been sovereign, but many people have not acknowledged God as their Lord. The sovereignty of God was declared in a new and powerful way in the life and ministry of Jesus.

### First Comes the Cross (v. 25)

The cross is the heart of God's purpose and the key to His kingdom.

### The Time of His Coming (vv. 26–30)

Jesus consistently taught the certainty of the fact of His coming but the uncertainty of the time.

### Effect on Present Actions (vv. 31–33)

The hope of the future coming affects present actions and values.

### Coming Judgment (vv. 34–37)

The future coming will involve judgment. Verses 34–35 refer to the separation of persons with close earthly ties but with different ultimate allegiances.

■ *God's kingdom would not be preceded by*
■ *signs that could be calculated and observed.*
■ *On the contrary, the kingdom was already*
■ *present in the coming of Jesus Christ. As for*
■ *the Son of Man's coming, it will be unex-*
■ *pected; and people will be unprepared.*

## QUESTIONS TO GUIDE YOUR STUDY

1. As followers of Christ, how are we to deal with brothers and sisters who sin against us?

2. What is the nature of true faith? What does Jesus mean by "increasing" our faith?

3. What effect should the fact of Jesus' imminent return have on us today?

## LUKE 18

### THE PARABLE OF THE UNJUST JUDGE (18:1–8)

This parable is closely connected to the preceding material by theme and audience, and it continues Jesus' teaching of the disciples. In the parable, two characters make up the picture: a persistent woman and an unjust judge. The woman is a widow who represents the needy, helpless, poor, and oppressed. She wanted help against an adversary. The judge finally agreed to vindicate her against her adversary. She annoyed him into granting her request. He had reached the stage where he would do anything to get her out of his hair.

The point of the parable is this: if the unjust judge finally grants the persistent widow's request, how much more will a just God hear and grant the petitions of His followers who pray to Him day and night?

The last question of the parable is somewhat puzzling. The intent of the question is not to raise doubts but to serve as a challenge from

"This judge was one of the paid magistrates appointed either by Herod or the Romans. Such judges were notorious. Unless a plaintiff had influence and money to bribe his way to a verdict, he had not hope of ever getting his case settled."

William Barclay, *The Gospel of Luke, 222.*

"If I felt my heart as hard as a stone; if I did not love God, or man, or woman, or little child, I would yet say to God in my heart, 'O God, see how I trust Thee, because Thou art perfect, and not changeable like me. I do not love Thee. I love noboby. I am not even sorry for it. Thou seest how much I need Thee to come close to me, to put Thy arm round me, to say to me, my child: for the worse my state, the greater my need of my Father who loves me. Come to me, and my day will dawn; my love will come back, and, oh! how I shall love Thee, my God! and know that my love is Thy love, my blessedness Thy being.'"

George MacDonald, in *Between Heaven and Earth*, ed. Ken Gire, (San Francisco: HarperCollins, 1997), 111–112.

Jesus to His followers to persevere in faith in the difficult times ahead.

■ *We do not need to "wear down" God until He*
■ *acts on our behalf. As a Father, He is sensi-*
■ *tive to our every need and ready to answer*
■ *our prayers.*

## THE PARABLE OF THE PHARISEE AND THE TAX COLLECTOR (18:9–14)

Within this parable we encounter a self-righteous Pharisee whose prayer in the Temple was essentially a self-eulogy. He thanked God that he was not like the others. In itself, the prayer could have been quite acceptable if the Pharisee was thanking God for protecting him from circumstances that might have led him to become a thief or adulterer. However, the Pharisee saw his not having succumbed to such sins as purely his own doing. There was no thanks for what God had done, but rather a long list of personal achievements. (Note the *I's!*).

In contrast, the tax collector demonstrated his attitude even by his physical stance. He stood "at a distance." His prayer sought God's mercy and forgiveness just like the psalmist (Ps. 51:1). The result, which would have been shocking for many of Jesus' listeners, was that the sinner who sought God's mercy left justified, not the Pharisee.

■ *In the parable of the Pharisee and the tax col-*
■ *lector, the Pharisee was so busy priding him-*
■ *self on his performance that he failed to*

- *realize he lacked the essential requirement of*
- *a right attitude. God relates to those people*
- *who have lost their pride and humbled them-*
- *selves in repentance.*

## JESUS' BLESSING OF THE CHILDREN (18:15–17)

Jesus teaches that one must receive God's kingdom like a little child. Jesus says the kingdom belongs to "such as these." Little children possess humility because they lack anything to boast of and can make no claim on God

## THE RICH RULER (18:18–30)

We find the story of the rich young ruler in all three synoptic Gospels, but only Matthew states that he was young. This ruler's concern was "to inherit eternal life."

Jesus saw that this man's whole life was wrapped up in his prosperity. He realized that only a complete renunciation would free this man to follow Him in the way of life that was abundant and eternal.

The rich man rejected the gospel, as he loved his possessions more than God and his neighbor.

### *Riches and the Kingdom (vv. 24–27)*

The ruler's rejection of the gospel was the occasion for Jesus' statement about the difficulty of a rich man entering the kingdom. The disciples were shocked at what Jesus said. The theology of the day interpreted wealth as a sign of God's favor.

### *Forsaking All for the Kingdom's Sake (vv. 28–30)*

Following the ruler's refusal to forsake all and follow Christ, Peter pointed out that he and the other disciples had done just that. Jesus

"Eye of a needle"

Attempts to understand this saying as involving a camel going through a small city gate (no evidence exists of a gate named *Eye of the Needle*) or as a mistranslation (*camel* as a mistranslation of the word *cable*) lose sight of the hyperbolic nature of Jesus' words. There is a rabbinic analogy that speaks of an elephant going through the eye of a needle, which is an example of the hyperbolic nature of Jesus' saying in verse 25. C. S. Lewis once observed that God *can* bring a camel through the eye of a needle but the camel will not to be the same creature having come through a needle's eye!

Three lessons from this event touch our lives:
1. One can be interested in eternal life without possessing it.
2. Many who claim to have obeyed God have done so only in a superficial sense.
3. The rich ruler lacked eternal life because he rejected Jesus' call for repentance.

assured Peter and the others that any sacrifice for the sake of the kingdom would be more than repaid.

■ *The rich ruler's life was wrapped up in his*
■ *prosperity. The Bible is clear that all of us*
■ *are in a plight from which we can be saved*
■ *only by the grace and power of God.*

## THE THIRD PASSION ANNOUNCEMENT (18:31–34)

This account involves Jesus' third passion prediction.

The disciples still do not comprehend what Jesus is saying.

## THE HEALING OF THE BLIND MAN AT JERICHO (18:35–43)

As Jesus approached Jerusalem, a blind man called out to Jesus from the roadside, "Jesus, Son of David, have mercy on me!" Others tried to silence him, but he refused to be quiet. Jesus heard his prayer and restored the blind man's sight.

Bartimaeus is an example of faith that refuses to give up. He showed great faith by responding to what he had heard, persisting in his request for help, and standing to his feet when Jesus summoned him. Bartimaeus then followed Jesus.

## QUESTIONS TO GUIDE YOUR STUDY

1. What is the point of the parable of the unjust judge?

2. What is it about childlike faith that Jesus commends? In what ways do we often complicate the matter of faith in our busy and complex lives?

3. The rich ruler rejected the gospel of Jesus Christ. What was his struggle? What might we learn from this tragic story?

## ZACCHAEUS, THE TAX COLLECTOR (19:1–10)

As Jesus passed through Jericho, the chief tax collector, Zacchaeus, sought to catch a glimpse of Him. Because of his short stature, he had to climb a tree. To his surprise, Jesus called him by name to come down, and together they went to Zacchaeus's home. Luke doesn't let us in on the conversation, but Zacchaeus emerged a changed man. He made two promises: (1) to give half of his possessions to the poor and (2) to pay back four times in cases where he had defrauded someone.

Jericho was seventeen miles east-northeast of Jerusalem. In Jesus' day it was famous for its balm (an aromatic gum known for its medicinal qualities). This along with its being the winter capital made it a wealthy city.

- *Zacchaeus showed the same determination to*
- *contact Jesus as Bartimaeus. He did not come*
- *to Jesus out of mere curiosity or with any*
- *skepticism but with an openness to Jesus'*
- *message. His spontaneous act of repentance*
- *revealed the work of grace in his heart and*
- *proved that he was now a son of Abraham.*

## THE PARABLE OF THE TEN MINAS (19:11–27)

The parable of the ten minas is also known as the parable of the pounds and is similar to the parable of the talents (Matt. 25:14–30). In the parable a noble man, about to be appointed king, gave ten servants each ten minas, which they were to "put to work" until the noble man returned as king. Luke's readers would have understood the noble man's absence to represent the time between the Ascension and the Second Coming of Christ.

Zacchaeus's restitution was far greater than it needed to be. "He shall confess his sins which he has committed, and he shall make restitution in full for his wrong, and add to it one-fifth of it, and give it to him whom he has wronged" (Num. 5:6–7, NASB).

Mina

The *shekel* was the basic unit of weight in the Hebrew system. Multiples of the *shekel* were the *mina* and the *talent*. A *talent* is estimated to have been about 3,000 *shekels* and a *mina* about 50 *shekels*. Although a *mina* was worth only about one-sixtieth of a *talent*, ten *minas* was still a significant amount as it represented about three months' wages.

"Rejoice greatly, O daughter of Zion! Shout in triumph, O daughter of Jerusalem! Behold,your king is coming to you; He is just and endowed with salvation, Humble, and mounted on a donkey, Even on a colt, the foal of a donkey" (Zech. 9:9, NASB).

When the noble man returned as king, he sent for the servants to learn what each had gained with his ten minas. He rewarded those who had been faithful and judged those who had been unfaithful.

- God entrusts believers with the gospel, and
- He wants them to multiply His message so
- the entire world will hear it. It is the obliga-
- tion of believers to be faithful stewards of the
- message He has entrusted to us until Jesus
- comes.

### THE MESSIANIC ENTRY INTO JERUSALEM (19:28–40)

Jesus now entered Jerusalem, His city of destiny.

He entered as the Messiah, but not as the Messiah whom many of His countrymen were seeking.

As Jesus approached Jerusalem, His following grew. As the procession reached a point where the city came into view, "the whole crowd of disciples began joyfully to praise God in loud voices for all the miracles they had seen." While Jesus was welcomed by many, He was criticized by the religious leaders.

### JESUS' LAMENT OVER JERUSALEM (19:41–44)

As Jesus approached Jerusalem, He wept over it, knowing the judgment would come in A.D. 70 when the Romans would destroy Jerusalem and the Temple.

## THE CLEANSING OF THE TEMPLE
## (19:45–48)

Jesus' cleansing of the Temple was an act of prophetic symbolism, not a sudden outburst of righteous indignation.

Jesus not only drove out the agents of the high priest, He proceeded to make the Temple court into the place for His daily teaching of the people.

■ *Official Israel failed to submit to God's rule.*
■ *This could only result in a visitation of divine*
■ *judgment, and, knowing that, Jesus wept for*
■ *Jerusalem.*

## QUESTIONS TO GUIDE YOUR STUDY

1. What lessons do we learn from the conversion of Zacchaeus?
2. What lessons about stewardship do we find in the parable of the ten minas? What can we do to be faithful stewards?
3. Why did Jesus choose to enter Jerusalem as He did?
4. What was Jesus' larger purpose in driving out the people who were selling animals in the Temple?

"'Behold, I am going to send My messenger, and he will clear the way before Me. And the Lord, whom you seek, will suddenly come to His temple; and the messenger of the covenant, in whom you delight, behold, He is coming,' says the LORD of hosts. 'But who can endure the day of His coming? And who can stand when he appears? For he is like a refiner's fire and like fullers' soap'" (Mal. 3:1–2, NASB).

## A QUESTION OF JESUS' AUTHORITY (20:1–8)

The religious leaders asked Jesus the source of authority for what He was doing. Their hope was that His answer would get Him into trouble with the Roman authorities.

Jesus refused to take the bait. Instead, He asked them a question: "Tell me, John's baptism—was it from heaven, or from men?" If they pleased the crowd by saying John was from God, the people would ask them why they did not believe John when he was alive. If they were to give their honest opinion that John was not a true prophet, the people might stone them.

■ *Hoping to trap Jesus, Jewish leaders ques-*
■ *tioned His authority for cleansing the Tem-*
■ *ple. Jesus refused to answer the question of*
■ *the Jewish leaders, and by doing so He*
■ *showed that their problem was not ignorance*
■ *but intentional opposition to God's will.*

## THE PARABLE OF THE WICKED TENANTS (20:9–19)

A man planted a vineyard and leased it to tenants. At harvest time, he sent servants, on three successive occasions, to collect some of the produce. The tenants beat the servants. Finally, the owner sent his own son. The tenants killed him.

Jesus asked His audience what the owner would do with the tenants and then answered His question by saying that the owner would kill the tenants and give the vineyard to others.

The teachers of the law and chief priests sought to arrest Jesus because they knew the tenants in the parable represented them. However, they were kept from carrying out their desire because of the people, who were supportive of Jesus.

■ *In the midst of the controversy regarding*
■ *Jesus' authority, He told a parable and asked*
■ *a question that gave an overview of God's*
■ *plan. They revealed God's commitment to*
■ *His Son despite Jewish rejection. The nation's*
■ *rejection would cost them. The kingdom*
■ *would go to new tenants.*

## A QUESTION ABOUT TRIBUTE TO CAESAR (20:20–26)

Some of the religious leaders approached Jesus and attempted to set Him up, first by flattery and then by asking Him a double-edged question. "Is is right to pay taxes to the Romans?"

Jesus knew that affirming the lawfulness of paying tribute to the Romans would alienate Him from the Jews. Denying the lawfulness of the tax would bring Roman wrath upon Him.

His answer sliced through the horns of the dilemma. When the Jewish leaders produced a coin in response to Jesus' request, they were undercutting their objection to the tax. Their use of the coin suggested a tacit acceptance of the emperor's authority. Jesus' logic was that the coin belonged to Caesar, and they should return to him his due.

The parable concludes with a quotation from Ps. 118:22 in which Jesus declares that He was God's foundation stone. God will establish His kingdom on Him, and He will be the focal point of judgment.

The tribute was an annual poll tax, which the Romans had begun to levy in A.D. 6. The imposition of this tax led to a Jewish rebellion under Judas the Galilean (see Acts 5:37). Romans required the payment of the tax with a special coin imprinted with a likeness of the emperor. Use of this special coin angered the Jews. Normal business activities used a copper coin without the image of the emperor.

■ *Christians must accept the state as ordained*
■ *by God and render respect and obedience to*
■ *the governments. When a conflict arises*
■ *between our allegiance to the state and our*
■ *allegiance to God, we must be true to God.*

## A QUESTION ABOUT THE RESURRECTION (20:27–40)

Luke now reports a second and final attempt by the leaders to confound Jesus in argument. This time the Sadducees, who are only mentioned here in Luke's Gospel, raise a far-fetched example.

Sadducees

"The Sadducees are mentioned here only in this Gospel. None of the Sadducee writings have survived so our information about the sect is fragmentary and we see the Sadducees only through the eyes of their opponents. . . . They were the conservative, aristocratic, high-priestly party, worldly-minded and very ready to co-operate with the Romans, which, of course, enabled them to maintian their privileged position."

Leon Morris, *The Gospel According to Saint Luke,* 289–290.

Telling a story of a woman who was married successively to seven siblings after each previous sibling spouse had died, the Sadducees asked Jesus, "At the resurrection, whose wife will she be, since the seven were married to her?" Their intent was to make the idea of the resurrection a joke.

In His response, Jesus presented two objections to their question.

They failed to understand the Scriptures and the power of God. Those who share in the resurrection will not marry.

■ *Jesus' answer to the Sadducees' question*
■ *revealed His unsurpassed wisdom and*
■ *knowledge. In contrast, the Sadducees failed*
■ *to understand the Scriptures. Jesus' oppo-*
■ *nents were forced to commend Him and*
■ *decided to cease further attempts to entrap*
■ *Him with His words.*

## A QUESTION ABOUT DAVID (20:41–44)

After His critics decided to ask no further questions, Jesus took the offensive and asked them a question about their designation of Messiah as the Son of David. He referred them to Ps. 110:1, the most frequently quoted Old Testament text in the New Testament, to show that the use of the title was inadequate and perhaps misleading as a guide to the Messiah's identity. Jesus pointed out that the Messiah was not a mere earthly replica of David but rather was David's Lord. He emphasized that the Messiah was divine as well as human.

"The LORD says to my Lord:
'Sit at My right hand,
Until I make Thine enemies a footstool for Thy feet'"

(Ps. 110:1, NASB).

## WARNINGS CONCERNING THE SCRIBES (20:45–47)

These verses describe religion at its worst. These leaders were using their religion to advance their own personal ambitions and to feed their pride.

## QUESTIONS TO GUIDE YOUR STUDY

1. What gave Jesus the authority to cleanse the Temple of those who were defiling it?
2. What is the lesson of the parable of the wicked tenants?
3. Jesus strongly denounced the hypocrisy of the scribes and Pharisees. What are parallels in today's religious structure that we as believers need to be aware of and quick to denounce?

"God's estimate of benevolence takes in not only what is given, but what is reserved."

George R. Bliss

## THE WIDOW'S OFFERING (21:1–4)

The widow in the Temple is the epitome of true religion, just as the scribes are the epitome of false religion.

The wealthy gave out of their abundance, and as a result, did not even miss it. By contrast, the widow gave all she had.

■ *God measures the gifts of His people not on*
■ *the basis of their size but on the basis of how*
■ *much remains.*

## THE DESTRUCTION OF THE TEMPLE (21:5–6)

As Jeremiah had prophesied the destruction of Solomon's Temple, so Jesus foretold the destruction of Herod's Temple. Many people in Jeremiah's day and in Jesus' day assumed that God would never allow His Temple to be destroyed or His people judged.

The Babylonians destroyed Solomon's Temple in 587 B.C. When Roman armies besieged Jerusalem in A.D. 70, the last fanatical defenders took refuge in the Temple. Eventually, the Romans overwhelmed them and leveled the Temple, as Jesus has predicted.

## SIGNS BEFORE THE END (21:7–11)

The disciples' questions (v. 7) focused on how they could know *when* the Temple would be destroyed. This event was associated in their minds with the end of the old order and the establishment of God's final kingdom. But

# Jesus' Discourse in Luke 21:7–36

| SECTION (VERSES) | TOPIC | KEY POINT |
|---|---|---|
| 7–11 | Signs before the end | Observable events will signal the coming judgment |
| 12–19 | Persecution of disciples | Many will suffer for their faith |
| 20–24 | Jerusalem's desolation | God will judge Jerusalem for its rejection of His purpose |
| 25–28 | Coming of the Son of Man | Christ's glorious return and the redemption of believers |
| 29–33 | Parable of the fig tree | Duty of watching for Christ's appearance |
| 34–36 | Exhortation to vigilance | Being prepared for His coming |

"Redemption"

The word *redemption* occurs only this time in Luke-Acts. For Luke, this probably means the *consummation of the hopes and promises for God's people*. His readers would no doubt think of this redemption as involving salvation in its fullest sense.

Redemption is the reason Christians can "stand up and lift up [their] heads." In the last days, they can be even more encouraged because their redemption is coming.

Jesus taught them that the "end will not come right away."

Jesus taught here that signs prior to the end include false teachers, a worsening world political situation, international crises, world-wide calamities, persecutions, and the preaching of the gospel.

## THE COMING PERSECUTION OF THE DISCIPLES (21:12–19)

Jesus predicted a time of intense persecution before the Temple would fall. He challenged His followers to see hostility not as a threat but as an opportunity for bearing testimony.

Verse 27 refers to the fulfillment of Dan. 7:13–14, 27. Jesus often referred to Himself as the Son of Man. Daniel describes how God would give the Son of Man sovereignty over all things. In a sense, this happened in connection with Jesus' life, death, and resurrection. In this sense, the kingdom is already a reality. In another sense, however, the present reality of the kingdom is recognized only through the eyes of faith. At Christ's future coming, the domination of godless nations will end and all people will become aware of the sovereignty of the Son of Man (Phil. 2:9–11).

## THE DESOLATION COMING UPON JERUSALEM (21:20–24)

These verses refer to the fall of Jerusalem, not the final coming of Christ. Having described what must take place before the destruction, Luke now describes the destruction itself.

## THE COMING OF THE SON OF MAN (21:25–28)

The vivid language of verses 25–26 symbolizes the giving way of the old order of creation to the new order of Christ's eternal kingdom. Jesus emphasized, however, not the signs themselves but the effect of these signs on humanity unprepared for Christ's coming.

- *The mustard seed has become a tree (13:19);*
- *the yeast has leavened the whole dough*
- *(13:21). The longings of Luke's readers are*
- *now realized to the fullest.*

## THE PARABLE OF THE FIG TREE (21:29–33)

This parable serves as a reassuring word for the preceding section about the Son of Man's coming. Even as the leafing of a fig tree announces the coming of summer, so the signs of 21:25–26 will announce and guarantee the Son of Man's coming.

The certainty of all this is assured by two emphatic elements:

1. The statement, "I tell you the truth" (v. 32).

2. The fact that the coming of the Son of Man is a more enduring promise than the existence of heaven and earth. The latter will pass away, but not Jesus' words.

In Luke, the events of the fall of Jerusalem are largely in view from verses 5–24. But those events are like those of the end.

## EXHORTATION TO VIGILANCE (21:34–36)

Since that day will come unexpectedly, disciples are to watch and be faithful. The events of A.D. 70 are a guarantee that the end will also come, since one set of events pictures the other.

## THE MINISTRY OF JESUS IN THE TEMPLE (21:37–38)

These verses form a concluding summary for the entire section on Jesus' ministry in Jerusalem.

Jesus' followers are to "be always on the watch" and "pray." Grammatically, this phrase is best understood as revealing the means by which one can be watchful: *Be always watchful by praying.*

■ *The Son of Man's return is guaranteed. Dis-*
■ *ciples of Jesus are to watch and pray and to*
■ *be faithful. In this way they can prepare for*
■ *His coming.*

## QUESTIONS TO GUIDE YOUR STUDY

1. What is the key lesson of the story of the widow's offering in the Temple?

2. Why did God allow the destruction of the Temple and the fall of Jerusalem? Might God still allow this kind of judgment today?

3. What is the point of the parable of the fig tree? What does the phrase *this generation* mean?

At this point, Luke's narrative shifts to his account of Jesus' passion. We have shifts in both scene (Temple to city) and content (teachings of Jesus to stories of Jesus). The passion consists of three parts, each containing unique events.

## Luke's Passion Narrative

| Event | Passage |
|---|---|
| *Part One:* | |
| Plot to betray and kill Jesus | 22:1–6 |
| The Last Supper | 22:7–23 |
| Teachings of Jesus | 22:34–38 |
| *Part Two:* | |
| Jesus' arrest | 22:39–53 |
| Jesus' trial | 22:54–23:25 |
| The crucifixion | 23:26–49 |
| Jesus' burial | 23:50–56 |
| *Part Three:* | |
| The resurrection and ascension of Jesus | 24:1–53 |

"Satan entered into Judas"

"That Satan entered into Judas, means that the devil, to accomplish his maglignant purposes against our Lord, took advantageof the wickedness of Judas, to direct him as a serviceable tool. Many other psychological explanations of the act of the traitor have been ingeniously attempted; but to carry them through without the supposition of Satanic agency has proved a sea of difficulty in which all have floundered—not swum."

George R. Bliss

### THE PLOT TO KILL JESUS (22:1–6)

The religious leaders already had plotted to kill Jesus. The plot became easier when one of His disciples offered to make Him available to the priests. Judas's willingness to betray Jesus simplified the task of the Sadducean priests. Fearing an arrest during the Passover feast might provoke a public revolt, they looked for an opportunity to make an arrest in secret.

## THE LAST SUPPER (22:7–38)

### *The Preparation of the Passover Meal (vv. 7–23)*

Luke portrays Jesus as an obedient Jew who kept the Law and celebrated the Passover. When the day arrived, Jesus sent Peter and John to prepare the Passover meal. Because Jesus was aware of Judas's plan to betray Him, He kept secret the place of the meal. Even Peter and John did not know where it was to be held until they arrived.

Their sign of the location was a man carrying a water jar, which was unusual since carrying water was considered women's work.

### *The Passover—Lord's Supper (vv. 14–20)*

In connection with His last Passover meal with the apostles, Jesus instituted the Lord's Supper, which like the Passover commemorated a divine deliverance and looked forward to the future consummation of God's kingdom. His words in verses 15–18 show that He saw this as His last meal with His followers before His suffering and death.

The Passover celebrated a past deliverance—God's deliverance of Israel from Egyptian bondage. Over the centuries it also came to be an anticipation of God's coming kingdom.

## Jesus' Farewell Discourse

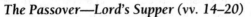

| SECTION | PASSAGE |
|---|---|
| Judas's betrayal of Jesus | 22:21–23 |
| Selfish desire for greatness | 22:24–30 |
| Peter's denial foretold | 22:31–34 |
| Misunderstanding of the nature of the kingdom | 22:35–38 |

### *Jesus' Betrayal Foretold (vv. 21–23)*

From God's point of view, the death of Jesus was God's plan for human redemption. However, those who were responsible for His death are held accountable for what they did. Judas was not a helpless pawn in a divine drama, or

81

**"Betray"**

Jesus' words of prediction at the Lord's Supper hold more meaning than a simple prediction of betrayal. The phrase *who is going to betray me* is active and forward-moving in its meaning. Grammatically, this phrase is a "present active participle," which means that the one betraying was "actually engaged in doing it"

A. T. Robertson, "Luke," *Word Pictures in the New Testament*, 268.

A literal translation would be *him who is in the process of betraying*. The betrayal had already begun (22:3–6).

"Therefore let him who thinks he stands take heed lest he fall" (1 Cor. 10:12, NASB).

Jesus would not have pronounced judgment on him for his betrayal.

### Greatness in the Kingdom (vv. 24–30)

A dispute over who was to be considered the greatest among the disciples become an occasion for Jesus to teach about true greatness in God's kingdom. Jesus contrasts the attitudes and values of the world with what it means to be great in God's kingdom.

### Peter's Denial Foretold (vv. 31–34)

All four Gospels predict Peter's coming three-fold denial. Luke alone refers to Satan's role in Peter's downfall. Even though Peter would experience great trials, Jesus indicated that He had prayed for Peter's faith to hold firm. Peter's answer showed that he comprehended neither the serious events fast approaching nor the reality of his own weakness.

### Two Swords (vv. 35–38)

This last account in Jesus' farewell discourse is not found in any of the other Gospels. Jesus contrasted the past mission of the disciples with the changed situation that was about to take place. On their early mission the disciples went out without provisions and depended entirely on the hospitality of their hearers. In the new situation brought about by Jesus' death, they must go equipped and be prepared to face hostility and persecution.

This involved their purchasing a "sword" because what the Scriptures said about the death of God's Son was about to be fulfilled. The opposition to Jesus that had been mounting was about to come to its culmination, and the end was very near. To Jesus' frustration, however, the disciples failed to grasp His meaning in the use of the sword metaphor, and He concluded the conversation.

■ *Jesus used His Last Supper with the disciples*
■ *as an occasion to deliver His farewell dis-*
■ *course. Although the disciples gained from*
■ *His teaching, they failed to grasp fully His*
■ *explanation of what was about to happen.*

## JESUS' ARREST (22:39–71)

Luke now directs his narrative to events surrounding Jesus' trial and crucifixion. The scene is now the Mount of Olives.

### The Prayer of Jesus (vv. 39–46)

The opening account in this new section involves Jesus' prayer on the Mount of Olives. He had taught the disciples that they needed to pray so their faith would not fail. They needed to pray, "Lead us not into temptation" (11:4). Their lack of prayer at this crucial time would help Luke's readers understand Peter's failure in the temptation that was to follow.

Luke's readers are again reminded that Jesus' suffering is at the heart of God's plan. His prayer clearly revealed that despite His own personal desire, He was submitting to the divine will, which involved the necessity of His death. His prayer served as a pattern for Luke's readers who might have to walk in the footsteps of their Lord.

### The Arrest of Jesus (vv. 47–53)

A crowd including Judas, the chief priests, and officers of the Temple guard, approached Jesus to arrest Him. John's account includes Roman soldiers as part of the crowd.

"Take this cup from me"

"Cup" is a metaphor for Jesus' suffering (Mark 10:38–39; Matt. 20:22–23). It is a metaphor in this passage not for physical death in general but for the particular death Jesus would suffer. "As He stood on the very brink of this awful experience His holy soul drew back from the horror of becoming the very essence of sin. If there were any other way by which man could be saved—but, if not, then He was ready for God's will to be done"

Herschel H. Hobbs, *An Exposition of the Gospel of Luke,* 312.

Before Jesus could stop him, one of His disciples cut off the ear of a servant of the high priest. Jesus rebuked His disciples and healed the servant.

Jesus then rebuked His opponents for their cowardice in not arresting Him openly while He taught in the Temple: "Am I leading a rebellion, that you have come with swords and clubs? Every day I was with you in the temple courts, and you did not lay a hand on me."

He also pointed out that this was the last desperate attempt of the power of darkness to thwart God's plan. What was taking place involved a far deeper opposition than that between the Jewish leadership and Jesus. It involved the cosmic opposition between Satan, the ruler of this age, and God. But God had permitted the opponents of His Son this hour. The power of darkness would be allowed to do what it wanted with Jesus. And so Jesus submitted to the will of the Father.

Although Peter's fall was lamentable, his repentance and subsequent service to Christ as recorded in Acts provides hope for all Christians.

### Peter's Denial of Jesus (vv. 54–62)

When Jesus was led away, Peter followed at a distance, and then on into the courtyard of the high priest. While in the courtyard, he was asked on three occasions whether he knew Jesus. Each time Peter denied that he knew Jesus. Then he remembered what Jesus had predicted. He then "went outside and wept bitterly."

### The Mocking of Jesus (vv. 63–65)

After His arrest, Jesus was mocked and suffered just as He had predicted. Because He was acknowledged as a prophet by other people, He was blindfolded and asked to identify who beat Him. The account ends with Jesus receiving further insults from His captors.

## *Jesus before the Sanhedrin (vv. 66–71)*

Jesus was next taken before the Sanhedrin.

The morning meeting was an attempt to legitimize what they already had decided to do. The Sanhedrin could not conduct a trial on a capital case at night. Also, this was not a trial at which evidence was being considered. The verdict was predetermined.

The Sanhedrin was a Jewish court of seventy members plus the high priest. They exercised authority over the religious life of the Jewish people. They also operated under the jurisdiction of the Roman authorities.

Looking to officially charge Him with blasphemy, the Sanhedrin tried to get Jesus to admit that He was the Messiah. "Are you then the Son of God?" they asked.

Jesus' reply was, "You are right in saying I am."

The leaders took Jesus' answer to their question as an affirmation and a claim to be the Christ, the Son of God. "We have heard it from his own lips." As far as Jesus' opponents were concerned, their purpose had now been achieved. It did not matter to them that Jesus was convicted on the basis of His own testimony, a patently illegal procedure.

- *Jesus' betrayal and arrest were the result of a*
- *plot carried out illegally by the religious*
- *authority. What was taking place involved a*
- *far deeper opposition than that between the*
- *Jewish leadership and Jesus. It involved the*
- *cosmic opposition between Satan, the ruler of*
- *this age, and God. And so Jeus submitted to*
- *the will of the Father.*

## QUESTIONS TO GUIDE YOUR STUDY

1. What is the significance of the Lord's Supper to present-day believers?

2. Review the message of Jesus' farewell discourse at the Last Supper. What was the disciples' attitude and response to His teaching? Which of Jesus' points did the disciples fail to grasp?

3. As you read Luke's account of Jesus agonizing in prayer before His arrest, what human emotions do you see? What does the account reveal about His relationship with the Father?

## LUKE 23

### JESUS' TRIAL (23:1–25)

#### *Jesus Before Pilate (vv. 1–5)*

The entire Sanhedrin brought Jesus to Pilate. The Sanhedrin had condemned Jesus for the sin of blasphemy. However, this was not a crime in the eyes of Rome.

## A Chronology of the Events of Jesus' Arrest and Trial

| EVENT | SOURCES WITHIN THE GOSPELS |
|---|---|
| 1. Jesus is arrested. | Mark-Matthew, Luke, John |
| 2. Jesus appears before Caiaphas. | John |
| 3. Jesus is "tried" by the Sanhedrin led by Caiaphas. | Mark-Matthew, Luke, John |
| 4. The Sanhedrin meets a second time to draw up official charges against Jesus to be presented before Pilate. | Mark-Matthew |
| 5. Jesus is led to Pilate. | Mark-Matthew, Luke, John |

Verse 2 spells out the accusations against Jesus: (1) subverting a nation; (2) opposing the payment of taxes to Caesar; and (3) claiming to be Messiah, that is, a king.

Focusing on only the third accusation, Pilate asked Jesus, "Are you the king of the Jews?"

Jesus responded, "Yes, it is as you say."

Pilate's verdict in verse 4 shows that he believed Jesus was innocent: "I find no basis for a charge against this man." (The information in vv. 4–5 is unique to Luke.) This should have been the official verdict, and the charges should have been dismissed. But the enemies were insistent and Pilate did not act decisively. When Pilate learned that Jesus was from Galilee, he tried to solve his dilemma by sending Jesus to Herod Antipas, tetrarch of Galilee and Perea.

Pontius Pilate was Roman governor of Judea from A.D. 26 to 37. His tenure as governor or prefect consisted of one provocation of Jewish sensibilities after another. In view of his record, it is a little surprising that Pilate allowed himself bo be pressured by Jewish leaders to crucify Jesus. One possible explanation is that he already felt his position was in jeopardy.

### Jesus Before Herod (vv. 6–12)
The account of Jesus' appearance before Herod is unique to Luke. This was the Herod who had imprisoned and killed John the Baptist. Herod thrilled at the prospect of seeing Jesus perform some sign, but Jesus refused to dignify him with any kind of reply. The evil ruler reacted by subjecting Jesus to cruel and humiliating mockery. He then sent Jesus back to Pilate without passing any sentence on His guilt or innocence.

Luke's purpose in recording this event is to provide a second ruler's testimony to Jesus' innocence.

### Pilate's Sentence (vv. 13–16)
Pilate interpreted Herod's actions to mean that Herod found Jesus innocent. Neither of these men, however, escaped guilt for their involvement in this shameful miscarriage of justice (Acts 4:27). Luke's readers are clearly told that

two rulers—the Roman governor Pontius Pilate and the tetrarch of Galilee, Herod Antipas—found Jesus innocent and wanted to release Him. Therefore, Jesus' crucifixion had nothing to do with personal guilt or culpability.

Pilate continued to seek Jesus' release. This time he sought to do so by allowing the people to choose, according to the custom, which "criminal" they wanted released. Pilate issued another strong statement about Jesus' innocence and then offered to have Him released. Roman law allowed for a prisoner to be beaten as a kind of warning for the future. Pilate hoped this compromise would satisfy Jesus' accusers.

### Jesus Delivered to Be Crucified (vv. 18–25)

To Pilate's dismay, the Jewish leadership and the people cried instead for the release of Barabbas. For the third time Pilate pronounced Jesus innocent and sought to release Him. The crowd kept shouting, "Crucify him! Crucify him!" Pilate was now intimidated by the Jewish leadership and the crowd. Finally, he passed judgment on Jesus. He released Barabbas to the people and handed over Jesus to their will.

■ *In spite of repeated pronouncements of His*
■ *innocence, Jesus was sentenced to die by cru-*
■ *cifixion. Jesus' opponents preferred the*
■ *release of a revolutionary and a murderer*
■ *rather than the one who "went about doing*
■ *good and healing" (Acts 10:38).*

### THE WAY TO THE CROSS (22:26–32)

Jesus was now led away from the presence of Pilate to the place of execution. On the way, Simon of Cyrene was commandeered to carry

Jesus' cross. As they proceeded, a great multitude of people followed. Among them were women, mourning and weeping over what was happening.

Jesus used this opportunity to pronounce that such mourning should not be directed toward Him but reserved for themselves. This incident, recorded only in Luke, points to the judgment coming on Jerusalem. A most terrible time of tribulation was coming upon them. In this poignant scene Jesus uttered a final prophetic warning of the judgment coming upon Israel.

■ *There is an illusion to what it means to be a*
■ *disciple. Being a disciple means to take up a*
■ *cross and follow Jesus. Simon of Cyrene was,*
■ *so to speak, the first person to take up his*
■ *cross and follow Jesus.*

## THE CRUCIFIXION (23:33–49)

The Romans reserved the horrors of crucifixion for criminals and slaves. This method of capital punishment was the first-century counterpart to firing squads and electric chairs.

### Jesus Crucified (vv. 33–38)

After Jesus arrived at Golgotha, the "place of the skull," He was crucified between two thieves. Crucifixion was a method of execution designed to torture and humiliate the victim. The Gospels do not focus on the torment Jesus endured, but on the significance of His death.

As He was crucified, Jesus prayed for the forgiveness of His opponents. Lots were cast and Jesus' garments were divided. While the people

**Death by Crucifixion**

Crucifixion was the method the Romans used to execute Christ. It was the most painful and degrading form of capital punishment in the ancient world. A person crucified in Jesus' day was first beaten with a whip consisting of thongs with pieces of metal attached to the end. This scourging was designed to hasten death and lessen the terrible ordeal. After the beating, the victim carried the crossbeam to signify that life was over and to break his will to live. A tablet detailing the crime was often placed around the criminal's neck. At the site, the prisoner was tied (normal method) or nailed (if a quicker death was desired) to the crossbeam. The nail would be driven through the wrist rather than the palm, since the smaller bones of the hand could not support the weight of the body. Pins or a small wooden block were placed halfway up the stake to provide a seat for the body lest the nails tear open the wounds or the ropes force the arms from their sockets.

watched, the rulers taunted Jesus, repeating some of His claims as being the Messiah.

The Gospels record seven sayings of Jesus on the cross. Two of Luke's sayings are prayers. As He was being crucified, He kept praying, "Father, forgive them, for they do not know what they are doing" (v. 34), and "Father, into your hands I commit my spirit" (v. 46).

## The Seven Sayings of Jesus on the Cross

| SAYING | PASSAGE | EXPLANATION |
| --- | --- | --- |
| 1. "Father, forgive them, for they do not know what they are doing." | Luke 23:34 | Jesus asked forgiveness for His enemies. |
| 2. "I tell you the truth, today, you will be with me in paradise." | Luke 23:43 | Jesus offered paradise to the repentant thief on the cross. |
| 3. "Dear woman, here is your son," and "Here is your mother." | John 19:27 | Jesus committed the care of Mary to his disciple John. |
| 4. "My God, my God, why have you forsaken me?" | Matt. 27:46 | Jesus was aware of His present alienation from God. |
| 5. "I am thirsty." | John 19:28 | Jesus expressed agony due to the torture of crucifixion. |
| 6. "It is finished." | John 19:30 | A cry of victory, expressing that He had paid the debt of sin. |
| 7. "Father, into your hands I commit my spirit." | Luke 23:46 | An expressed confidence in the triumphant restored fellowship with the Father after death. |

## The Two Criminals (vv. 39–43)

The incident of the two criminals raises the question of why some people believe and some don't. Both criminals apparently had been exposed to the same sights and sounds; yet one joined in the mockery of Jesus, and the other believed. The one who believed asked to be remembered in Christ's coming kingdom. Jesus promised him that he would be with Jesus in paradise on that very day.

Two other men, both criminals, were led out with Jesus. This fulfilled the prophecy of Isa. 53:12, which says of the Suffering Savior, He "was numbered with the transgressors. For he bore the sin of many."

## The Death of Jesus (vv. 44–49)

The eerie darkness of Jesus' final hours pointed to the cosmic significance of His dying. The cry recorded by Matthew (27:46) and Mark (15:34) showed that the forces of darkness did their worst to Jesus during that time. The prayer in verse 46 showed that Jesus had won the victory. At the time the disciples did not realize this, but after the resurrection they saw the cross in a totally new light.

"Paradise"

This is an old Persian term meaning literally "enclosure" or "wooded park." All three New Testament references, including this one, refer to the abode of the righteous dead. Over the years, it came to refer to heaven.

The dead in Christ share with the living this hope of the final consummation of God's redemptive purpose.

The tearing of the Temple curtain signified that the death of Christ had opened the way for all people into the presence of God. Knowing that He had completed His departure, Jesus committed His spirit into His Father's hands: "Father, into your hands I commit my spirit." And then He breathed His last breath.

The response of the Roman centurion is the account's high point, serving as the final witness to Jesus' innocence. The centurion was convinced that Jesus was innocent and praised God.

■ *Even in His crucifixion Jesus was in control*
■ *of all that was taking place. All was happen-*
■ *ing in accordance with the fulfillment of His*
■ *teachings and plans. No one took His life*
■ *from Him. He gave it freely.*

## THE BURIAL OF JESUS (23:50–56)

### Joseph of Arimathea (vv. 50–53)

Joseph's act was a sign of hope. As a member of the Sanhedrin, he opposed what that group had done. Now he acted with faith and courage to provide a tomb for the body of Jesus.

### The Women (vv. 54–56)

These verses bridge the gap between Luke's accounts of the crucifixion and resurrection of Jesus. These loyal women had ministered to Him in life. They were determined to do what they could for Him after He was dead.

## QUESTIONS TO GUIDE YOUR STUDY

1. Throughout His trial, Jesus was seen as innocent by the authorities; yet He allowed Himself to be sentenced and executed. Why did He not contest these proceedings?

2. Evaluate the character of Pontius Pilate as presented in Luke's account. What were his convictions? What ultimately drove his decision making?

3. What is the significance of the suffering which Christ endured on the cross? What does His death and resurrection mean to those who believe on Him?

# LUKE 24

This chapter deals with the resurrection and ascension of Jesus. In this section, we find the culmination of all that has gone before. Luke divides this section into five accounts. None of the Gospels records all the resurrection appearances of Jesus. Each evangelist tells of the resurrection in light of his distinctive purpose. Luke emphasizes the reality of the resurrection and the difference it made in the lives of the disciples.

## THE WOMEN AT THE EMPTY TOMB (24:1–12)

Carrying spices they had prepared, Mary Magdalene, Joanna, and Mary the mother of James went to visit the tomb of Jesus. They were greeted with a shock. They found the stone rolled away and the tomb empty. In their perplexity they heard two angels announce that Jesus was not dead, but alive! However, when they reported this to the apostles, they did not believe them. Some of the men went to the tomb and found it empty.

The angels reminded the women that Jesus had predicted His death and resurrection. How could the disciples have heard those predictions and not be expecting Jesus to be raised from the dead? Apparently, they had heard only what they expected to hear.

## JESUS' APPEARANCE ON THE ROAD TO EMMAUS (24:13–35)

Only Luke records this appearance of Jesus to two of His followers on the road to Emmaus. In fact, this is one of three accounts of post-resurrection appearances unique to Luke.

Emmaus

"Emmaus" means "hot baths." It was a village about sixty furlongs (seven miles) from Jerusalem. As many as four sites have been proposed as the locaton of Emmaus, but certainty isn't possible.

These men on their way to Emmaus spoke frankly with Jesus but did not recognize Him. Their conversation revealed how Jesus' friends were feeling before they became aware of His resurrection. They revealed their feelings not only by their words but also by how they looked: "They stood still, their faces downcast" (v. 17).

Jesus then led the two into a discussion. Many people of Jesus' day were diligent students of the Scriptures, but most missed the central message. They focused their attention on the passages that presented the Messiah as a glorious King, but they missed the passages that spoke of suffering as God's way of dealing with evil. The risen Lord, still unrecognized by the two Emmaus disciples, proceeded to show them how this theme runs through the Old Testament (v. 27). He showed them that the suffering of the cross is the way of triumph.

**Jesus' Resurrection Body**

The exact nature of Jesus' resurrection body remains a mystery. He appeared to the disciples from time to time, usually suddenly. On the other hand, He had a body that could be seen and touched, and the disciples recognized the body as Jesus' body. The resurrection of Jesus, therefore, means more than that Jesus' spirit survived death. It points to two great truths of Christianity: (1) the tomb was empty; and (2) people saw Jesus alive in bodily form.

The day was almost over when the two men recognized Jesus. He then miraculously disappeared from their sight. Their certainty in knowing who Jesus was came in the sharing of Scripture and the "breaking of bread." They now knew why their hearts had burned within them as they walked along the way.

## JESUS' APPEARANCE TO THE DISCIPLES IN JERUSALEM (24:36–43)

The disciples, fearing persecution from the authorities, had met behind locked doors.

Jesus suddenly and supernaturally appeared to them. If the disciples believed Jesus was risen, why were they startled and frightened when Jesus appeared to them? Hearing Peter's testimony was one thing, but suddenly being confronted by the Lord was something else. Jesus challenged them to look carefully and to touch Him. He even ate a piece of fish to show them He was not a ghost.

Even as Jesus spoke to them, the disciples "still did not believe it because of joy and amazement" (v. 41).

## JESUS' COMMISSION TO THE DISCIPLES (24:44–49)

Having assured the disciples of His physical resurrection, Jesus then gave them His final instructions. As with the two disciples on the road to Emmaus, He explained to them what is written in the Scriptures. To fulfill the Scriptures, something else must be accomplished. It involved the preaching in Jesus' name of repentance for the forgiveness of sins to all the world, beginning in Jerusalem.

The disciples were to be Jesus' witnesses, and they were to proclaim what they themselves had seen and heard. First, however, they were to wait in Jerusalem until Jesus sent the promise of His Father so they would be divinely empowered to fulfill this mission. In two other Gospels, as well as in the longer ending of Mark, there exists some form of a final commissioning scene (Matt. 28:19–20; John 20:21–23; Mark 16:15–16).

■ *This entire chapter has focused on the disci-*
■ *ples' role as eyewitnesses of Jesus' ministry,*
■ *death, and resurrection. They were directed*
■ *to share their personal experience of the*
■ *risen Christ.*

## THE ASCENSION (24:50–53)

These verses are a short account of the Ascension, which is also described in Acts 1:9–11.

Leaving Jerusalem, Jesus led the disciples to Bethany on the Mount of Olives. After bestowing upon them His parting blessing, He was taken up into heaven. The striking part of this account is what happened after Jesus left the disciples. Having worshiped Jesus, the disciples returned with great joy to Jerusalem.

**The Significance of the Ascension of Christ**

The Ascension concluded Jesus' earthly ministry. It allowed eyewitnesses to see both the risen Christ on earth and victorious, and the eternal Christ returning to heaven to minister at the right hand of the Father. Moreover, the Ascension expanded Christ's ministry from its geographically limited earthly dimensions to its universal heavenly dimensions.

Earlier, when Jesus had been taken from them by death, they were completely demoralized. But now, after being assured of His resurrection, they were able to rejoice even though He had departed from them. What better could show the difference made by their confidence in the resurrection of Jesus Christ from the dead!

■ *The question "Who is Jesus?" is now fully*
■ *answered. The disciples' worshiping Jesus*
■ *was an acknowledgment of His divinity.*

## QUESTIONS TO GUIDE YOUR STUDY

1. What was the scene at the tomb of Jesus when the women arrived? What was the reaction of the women? What would have been your reaction?

2. When the two disciples on the road to Emmaus finally recognized who Jesus was, what confirmed His identity? What lessons might we draw from this event?

3. For what reasons did Jesus make His several post-resurrection appearances? In what ways does His ministry continue?

4. Jesus' disciples carried out their commission having been eyewitnesses of Jesus' ministry, death, and resurrection. On what basis do His followers today carry on the Great Commission?

The following list is a collection of the works used for this volume. All are from Broadman & Holman's list of published reference resources. They are listed here to accommodate the reader's need for more specific information concerning the Gospel of Luke. All of these works will greatly aid in the reader's study, teaching, and presentation of the message of Luke. The accompanying annotations can be helpful in guiding the reader to the proper resources.

Adams, J. McKee, revised by Joseph A. Callaway, *Biblical Backgrounds*. This work provides valuable information on the physical and geographical settings of the New Testament. Its many color maps and other features add depth and understanding.

Blair, Joe, *Introducing the New Testament*, pp. 81–90. Designed as a core textbook for New Testament survey courses, this volume helps the reader in understanding the content and principles of the New Testament. Its features include maps and photos, outlines, and discussion questions.

Cate, Robert L., *A History of the New Testament and Its Times*. An excellent and thorough survey of the birth and growth of the Christian faith in the first-century world.

Dean, Robert J., *Luke* (Layman's Bible Book Commentary, vol. 17). A popular-level treatment of Luke. This easy-to-use volume provides a relevant and practical perspective for the reader.

*Disciple's Study Bible*, pp. 1268–1311. This is a study Bible designed to help Christians grow as disciples. It involves them in a study of twenty-seven great truths of the Christian faith. The notes and commentary inspire readers to discover how their beliefs can be applied to their lives.

*Holman Bible Dictionary* An exhaustive, alphabetically arranged resource of Bible-related subjects. An excellent tool of definitions and other information on the people, places, things, and events.

*Holman Bible Handbook,* pp. 585–605. A comprehensive treatment that offers outlines, commentary on key themes and sections, and full-color photos, illustrations, charts, and maps. Provides an accent on the broader theological teachings.

*Holman Book of Biblical Charts, Maps, and Reconstructions*, pp. 95–97, 101. A colorful, visual collection of charts, maps, and reconstructions. These well-designed tools are invaluable to the study of the Bible.

Stein, Robert H., *Luke* (The New American Commentary, vol . 24).

Lea, Thomas D., *The New Testament: Its Background and Message*, pp. 143–280. An excellent resource for background material—political, cultural, historical, and religious. Provides background information in both broad strokes on specific books, including the Gospels.

Robertson, A. T., *A Grammar of the Greek New Testament in the Light of Historical Research*. An exhaustive, scholarly work on the underlying language of the New Testament. Provides advanced insights into the grammatical, syntactical, and lexical aspects of the New Testament.

Robertson, A. T., *Word Pictures in the New Testament*, "Luke," vol. 2. This six-volume series provides insights into the language of the New Testament Greek. Provides word studies as well as grammatical and background insights into Luke.

# SHEPHERD'S NOTES

# SHEPHERD'S NOTES